PRAISE FOR *KING JESUS AND THE BEAUTY OF OBEDIENCE-BASED DISCIPLESHIP*

I rarely read books about the kingdom of God that make me cry. But then, this is just what David Young does. His stories drive home a well-crafted theology that is moving and practical. David paints pictures that make things I deeply believe much more vivid. I found reading it such a pleasure, it penetrated my soul.

—**BILL HULL,** leader, The Bonhoeffer Project;
writer; discipleship evangelist

David Young is a unique blend of scholar and pastor, with a mission to make biblical disciples in relational environments. In this book he blends his passion for the Word of God, as it has been understood historically, with practical truths so needed today if we are truly to fulfill the mission the Lord has given his church. I am so grateful for people like him who still really preach the gospel as it was taught and received in the beginning. So many are watering down the word of God, but David doesn't. We need more of these voices. I recommend this book and also listening to David speak whenever he does.

—**JIM PUTMAN,** cofounder and senior pastor,
Real Life Ministries; author, *Church Is a Team Sport*,
Real-Life Discipleship, and *The Power of Together*

Exponential is passionate about seeing movements of healthy reproducing communities of faith. Obedience-based disciple making, as David Young so simply and thoughtfully unpacks it in this excellent practical theological guide, is the key. Unfortunately, it may be the most important priority missing in the Western church. Thank you, David, for having the courage to write this book. I get excited thinking about the impact we'll see if the next generation of church planters embraces and lives out the principles and truths you've so thoughtfully articulated for us.

—**TODD WILSON,** president and CEO, Exponential

I was stirred reading this book—a timeless and much-needed call to Jesus followers, particularly for Christians in the Western church (like me) who can often be steeped in an individualistic, consumer-minded type of faith. May our lives be one of willing surrender and obedience to the rightful King of Kings and Lord of Lords: King Jesus.

—**DREW HYUN,** church planting catalyst; pastor, Hope Church NYC

Rarely does such street-level, livable wisdom and academic acumen meet in one book. David Young brings to the surface an obvious yet little practiced core of Jesus' training of his disciples. As church leaders go through fits and starts trying to find Jesus' secret sauce, Young gently but brilliantly points out the obvious: Jesus called his followers to obedience. This book is a must-read because if you miss Young's simple yet profound point, you'll miss the essential message of Jesus.

—**ROY MORAN,** spiritual literacy catalyst

In 2003, a successful megachurch pastor, David Young, came home from a season of prayer asking God for a clear vision for the church to engage. God has honored that vision in seven amazing years of new fruitfulness. And David's new book illuminates how Jesus' kingdom values and practices transform whole communities. Whether you are a theologian, a minister, a missionary, or an ordinary Christ follower who wants to be an extraordinary disciple, this book may be one of the best you will read this year.

—**JERRY TROUSDALE,** director of international ministries, New Generations; cofounder, Final Command; missionary; pastor; author

David takes the reader through a deep reconnection to the purpose and beauty of the gospel message of Jesus. It reminds, or maybe educates for the first time, the simple yet profoundly important principles of submission and dedication that every believer should be pursuing. This book is digestible, practical, deep, and gives the reader a breathtaking view of the lordship of our creator.

—**COREY TRIMBLE,** founder and lead pastor, The Experience Community Church

This book is an easy and encouraging read. It is filled with powerful examples and heart-touching stories. You will be encouraged in a fresh way by the impact King Jesus can have in your life and in the lives of your friends. I commend it to you.

—DR. DANN SPADER, author, *Four Chair Discipling* and *Walk Like Jesus*

A consuming loyalty to King Jesus. This is our heart's cry for ourselves and for others. But the struggle is real. We need fresh fire. Using Scripture, story, and practical wisdom, David Young shows how to ignite allegiance to the King of Kings so that it can spread like wildfire.

—MATTHEW W. BATES, author, *Gospel Allegiance*; Associate Professor of Theology, Quincy University

This book is a master thriller. It tells us not only about the kingship of Jesus in our lives but also how Jesus is king of the universe. On every page, David Young is practical, realistic, and very honest. What beats me is not how he accept his mistakes and failures but how he prays to King Jesus to set them right. This book will cross a major threshold in saving souls for King Jesus.

—SHODANKEH JOHNSON, global leader of disciple-making movements, New Harvest Ministries

Obedience. It's how Jesus walked with his Father. In this book, David Young refreshingly reveals Jesus to us through his kingship and kingdom, his lordship and discipleship, and the need for us to daily incorporate his presence and teachings into our lives. Reading David's book will revive a passion for Jesus and his kingdom within you, as well as a desire to walk in obedience just like him.

—DAVE BUEHRING, founder and president, Lionshare

KING
JESUS

AND THE BEAUTY OF
OBEDIENCE-BASED DISCIPLESHIP

KING JESUS

AND THE BEAUTY OF
OBEDIENCE-BASED DISCIPLESHIP

DAVID YOUNG

ZONDERVAN REFLECTIVE

King Jesus and the Beauty of Obedience-Based Discipleship
Copyright © 2020 by David M. Young

Requests for information should be addressed to:
Zondervan, *3900 Sparks Dr. SE, Grand Rapids, Michigan 49546*

ISBN 978-0-310-53775-5 (softcover)

ISBN 978-0-310-53777-9 (audio)

ISBN 978-0-310-53776-2 (ebook)

Cover design: Tammy Johnson
Cover art: © PureSolution / Shutterstock
Interior design: Kait Lamphere

Printed in the United States of America

20 21 22 23 24 25 26 27 28 29 30 /LSC/ 18 17 16 15 14 13 12 11 10 9 8 7 6 5 4 3 2 1

CONTENTS

FOREWORD

Seven years ago, I received a phone call from David Young. I was at home, and he apologized for calling me on a Saturday, asking whether he was interrupting anything. He was leading a church, and he asked me to coach him in making a shift to a disciple-making focus.

When calls like this come, I typically say no, either because I'm too busy or because I don't align with the theological posture of the person asking. I had recently invested a decade of my life working with leaders who were not on the same page with me theologically, and I was not going to do it again.

Having grown up in a Western Canadian truck driver's family, I can be a bit blunt sometimes. So I cut to the chase and blurted out my pin-you-in-the-corner questions. I expected David's answers would confirm my suspicions and I could end the conversation with a simple, "I am sorry, but I cannot help you."

David paused. Then, in a you're-not-going-to-like-my-answer kind of way, he shared his convictions. Then, I paused. His answers were the opposite of what I had expected him to say, and the opposite of what he thought I would want to hear! In that moment of honest surprise, we were hooked. I agreed to coach him, and he later began to coach me as well.

It was one of the best decisions I ever made.

In just a moment I am going to circle back and tell you why David, as a person, is a great guide for you. But let me start with several reasons why you will want to read his book:

- It is easy to read and filled with lots of great stories.
- It provides a solid exposition of Matthew 28:18–20 (the Great Commission).
- It gives a very good summary of the biblical teaching on the kingdom of God.
- It explains obedience-based discipleship better than any other resource I can find.
- It focuses on helping you to grasp the wonder, grandeur, and majesty of Jesus as king.
- It can change your life and the lives of the people in your church.

In short, it will inform your mind, enflame your spirit, and supercharge your will. It will help you to be a disciple who makes disciples.

If you are looking for a practical guide, then you have found the right book. However, if you gravitate toward the practical and like to steer clear of theological reflection, there is one challenge you may face as you read it. I want you to know it in advance so you will persevere through it. It is chapter 2, titled "Jesus Christ, King of the Universe." David earnestly wrestled with this chapter. He knew that the content was essential but that some people might get bogged down in it and lose a little enthusiasm. It may be challenging content, but it is the theological foundation of the book.

Think of this book as a really good meal. In such a meal, you will have some food that is easy to eat and delightful to taste. Another part of the meal is the food that might still taste good, but more important, it is really good for you and essential to good health. Chapter 2 is that kind of food. Read it that way. It provides good theology and helps you to grasp the substance of the Word of God.

The thesis of the book is seeing the theological beauty that Jesus has come as king of the universe. Those who give their allegiance to Jesus as saving king and trust and follow him in obedience-based discipleship find the best life anyone could ever live. This book will change your perspective on Jesus and obedience.

Here at Discipleship.org, we champion Jesus-style disciple making. We bring together leading disciple-making networks, speakers, writers, practitioners, and leaders. I have the privilege of being the point leader of Discipleship.org, which means that I have the responsibility to prayerfully find and promote the best disciple-making voices for others to follow. We seek to promote these voices through our national disciple-making forums, ebooks, podcasts, newsletters, courses, webinars—and in print books through our Discipleship.org Resource series. I am grateful for Zondervan's partnership with this book (and others) for our resource library. David Young and his ministry are exemplary of all we promote.

Now, back to why I wholeheartedly recommend David as your guide in obedience-based discipleship and why he is uniquely qualified to write this book. Here are five things I want you to know about him:

1. He walks closely with God privately and publicly, with great integrity.
2. He is a disciple maker who effectively leads a disciple-making church.
3. He is a brilliant biblical scholar with a PhD from Vanderbilt University (the "Harvard of the South").
4. His church is crazy in love with him as a speaker and leader (for good reason).
5. His wife and adult children—who know him better than anyone— think that he hung the moon in the sky.

This book provides the background narrative (or theological foundation) that David used to lead a traditional megachurch through an effective transition to a disciple-making church.

David Young is a very good guide. And this book is a *very* good read.

—*Bobby Harrington,* point leader for
Discipleship.org and Renew.org

ACKNOWLEDGMENTS

Before we dive in, allow me to say a brief thank you to Bobby Harrington, who challenged me to write this book. Bobby has been a mentor of mine for years now. He taught me what discipleship can look like. I consider him a great friend and a brilliant coach.

I also wish to thank my editor Ryan Pazdur and the team at Zondervan, including Nathan Kroeze. I also thank Daniel Frampton for his kind suggestions for improving the book. Zondervan has had an enormous influence in my life for many years. What a privilege to work with the company on this project!

I also want to thank my church, North Boulevard, for letting me live out my faith in a loving, encouraging, and risk-taking community. For nearly a quarter of a century, the members of my congregation have been a tremendous blessing to me. We've had a wonderful ride together in following King Jesus. They are really good people. And you'll hear from a number of them as you read this book.

I also thank my anonymous team of young proofreaders, who, early on, offered me valuable critiques that helped me change the course of the book.

All of the stories in this book are about real events and real people unless otherwise indicated. To protect the privacy of people in these stories, I have sometimes altered and generalized certain details, which I believe I have done without betraying the essence of the story. Where the story gets specific, I have secured permission from those involved before telling it.

And now I must thank my family, each of whom also appears in this book. I especially want to thank my son, Jonathan, who appears frequently. It took great courage and love for him to give me permission to share some of these stories. May his courage be a blessing for many. Jonathan David Young, you are my hero.

About me: I have only one mental channel. It's sometimes a blessing, such as when we need intense focus on a difficult subject. But it's often a curse. It can keep me anxious, distracted, and distant even when I don't intend to be. Julie, Rachel, and Jonathan are among the greatest blessings I have ever had. They have put up with me for a long, long time. I thank God for them, and I thank them for tolerating me, even loving me.

I also thank them for allowing me to use them, over and over again, as illustrations for my obsessive writing and speaking projects. You'll hear more about them in the book.

Finally, I thank my king. I apologize to you, King Jesus, for the times I was not faithful to you; I apologize for my sins and my acts of rebellion. I ask for your grace. And I commit myself again to trusting and following you, *my* king.

"Blessed is the king who comes
in the name of the Lord!"
"Peace in heaven and glory in the highest!"
—LUKE 19:38

CHAPTER 1

JESUS IS A BETTER KING THAN I'LL EVER BE

On his robe and on his thigh he has this name written:

KING OF KINGS AND LORD OF LORDS.

—REVELATION 19:16

I want a faith like this.

My son, Jonathan, and I were taking a road trip from Kansas City, where I was living at the time, to Branson, Missouri. He was only a small boy. We wanted to see a few of the shows, ride the rides, and explore the shops.

We were headed down Highway 71 in a driving rain. Suddenly and without warning, my car hydroplaned on the four-lane, divided highway, which is now an interstate. If you've ever lost control of your car at seventy miles per hour, you can guess what I felt. If you've ever lost control of your car, spiraled around the highway, crossed the median, and saw yourself headed straight toward an eighteen-wheeler coming directly at you, you can guess with even more certainty what I felt. And if you've ever done these things with your eight-year-old son in the front seat next to you—well, you get the point.

We careened across the grassy median, still turning in circles. We emerged onto the other side of the highway, sliding now headfirst toward oncoming traffic. I think I yelled, but I don't remember for sure. Then, when we were just yards from a fatal collision with a giant truck, our rear tire caught the edge of the pavement, and we were slung back down into the slick, grassy median. We spun around a few more times and came to a stop.

I sat there, stunned and shocked. I could taste my heart in the back of my throat.

After a few seconds, I looked over at my son. He was looking back at me wide-eyed and with a big grin on his face. "Daddy," he said, "that was fun! Let's do it again."

I want that kind of faith.

Let's face it. Life is a ride—sometimes fun, sometimes mundane, and sometimes terrifying. We often try to travel it alone, using our limited instincts as guides. But it doesn't have to be this way, for there is one who offers to direct our lives in the richest way possible. He offers us hope, love, purpose, and a spiritual adventure beyond anything we can imagine. He has numerous names in the Bible.

We'll call him King Jesus.

The thesis of this book is that Jesus has come as the king of the universe, and he invites us to enter his kingdom, respond in obedient discipleship, and live in his powerful presence.

And King Jesus is a better king than you or I will ever be. If we insist on driving our lives, it might go okay for a while, but eventually they careen out of control. And we'll never go far. We'll miss the scenery. We'll never feel the power. And we'll not arrive at our eternally appointed destination.

We are accustomed to calling Jesus "Savior." And we should be. He does save us from our sins, our guilt, and our failures. We are also accustomed to calling him "Christ"—the most common designation for Jesus in Scripture. And he is the Christ, the Anointed One of Israel who gives the entire world all the hope it needs. We are used to calling Jesus "Son of God," a designation that means, among other things, that he is divine. And Jesus is God, so we are right to call him this.

But until recently, many North Americans had not learned to call Jesus "King." That's beginning to change, thanks to the brilliant work of such scholars as N. T. Wright and Scot McKnight, who have helped a generation focus on the kingdom work of Jesus as king.[1]

Calling Jesus "King" is not a mere theological claim; it has implications for how we live. It is not just a title. Kingship denotes a position, and a very real position with very real and eternal consequences. If Jesus is king, we have only two choices in response. We can rebel against him, raise puppet kings, construct our own kingdoms, and generally thumb our noses at him, or we can submit to him in obedience-based discipleship.

This book is a call for us to recognize the Jesus who is king and submit to him in obedience-based discipleship. And the subject is sorely needed, for we must be honest with ourselves about how poorly things are going with us as kings. With you in charge, how is your life going? How are your relationships? How are your levels of anxiety and fear? How much shame do you feel? How well do you sleep at night? How's your marriage? Your prayer life? Your levels of peace, joy, and happiness?

Could it be that you are still sitting on the throne of your life, treating King Jesus as a mere advisor? Or worse, is King Jesus a puppet who serves your interests but makes no real demands on you?

What would change in your life if you started treating Jesus as nothing short of the king of the universe? I mean this not only for those of you who do not currently follow Jesus but also for those of you who are believers but have stopped short of handing your life over to King Jesus. I invite you who do not currently follow him to look over the fence into the lives of those who have fully submitted to the kingship of Jesus and see the beauty of following him. I invite those of you who are stuck halfway in your faith to go all in—to crucify yourself so you can enjoy a life in which Christ now lives in you (Gal. 2:20). I'm inviting all of you to crown Jesus king of your life.

North Americans don't think much about kings. After all, we fought a war nearly 250 years ago to escape royalty. We prefer democracy. We like our republic, a term that means something like "the people are the thing." But it's worth asking how well making ourselves the thing is working. How's it working for our planet? How's it working for our politics? Is this a peaceful world? Is it a flourishing world? Are people treating each other right? Are we happy?

Here's a radical proposal taken straight from the Scriptures: Jesus is the king of the universe, and if you crown him king of your life—not only in word but in fact—everything will change for you. Everything!

So I invite you into a radical relationship with Jesus as your king. I will argue that because Jesus is king of the universe, the right response to him is obedience-based discipleship. We crown Jesus king of our lives when we have the faith to respond to him with full obedience. People become disciples of Jesus when they, as King Jesus says, deny themselves and take up their crosses daily and follow him (Luke 9:23).

But I know that I'm up against several obstacles.

First, I'm up against some very bad models of King Jesus. Because many of us want to remain king of our lives, we tend to create Jesuses who will agree with our desires and fit our worldviews. We create Jesuses who affirm our sinfulness, who would never correct us, much less judge us. We want a Jesus who merely teaches us to look deep within and find ourselves, who gives us a good place to raise our children, or who affirms our flimsy traditions about worship or whatnot. Many of us have created imposter Jesuses. This makes obedience to King Jesus impossible because we have distorted him to the point that we no longer know who he is. One of the first tasks before me is to tear down the imposters so that we can see clearly the real Jesus. It's only then that we can obediently follow him.

Second, I'm up against some bad theology. Many North Americans have been taught that obedience is a bad word. Our culture prizes authenticity over obedience. Many consider obedience to be a form of conformity or even enslavement. Even worse, some Christians have been taught that obedience is a work and therefore must never be connected to salvation. Imagine this: the New Testament clearly says that Jesus himself was obedient and thereby became "the source of eternal salvation for all who obey him" (Heb. 5:9). But entire churches today argue that obedience is the opposite of faith and therefore unnecessary.

At the same time, many of us grew up in legalistic churches and denominations. We were essentially taught that no matter how good we are, we will never be good enough. In these churches, obedience is not a loving response to a gracious God; it is a moral and ritualistic to-do list used to judge, condemn, and marginalize people. These churches confuse the beauty of obedience with having a harsh, judgmental spirit. They teach a works-based salvation in which nobody is ever good enough. Those who grew up in such churches have often internalized guilt, shame, and failure and walked away from King Jesus, or—nearly as bad—reduced the beauty of his kingdom to a list of rules used to condemn everybody else.

But let's be honest. The third and most persistent problem I'm up against is the selfishness that lives in our hearts. We may have fuzzy Jesuses and bad theology, but for most of us the real problem is that we want to crown ourselves as king of the universe. Sure, we want Jesus around when we need him, but most of us have a terrible time getting off the thrones of our hearts so King Jesus can take his seat. Most of us want to be king, and we are mad that we are not.

And so we cheat King Jesus, lie to him, steal from him, hold back from him, refuse to trust him, and make excuses when we disobey him, all so we can keep ourselves on the throne. Many of us do that even while presenting ourselves to the world as his humble servants. But the dissonance between our pretending that Jesus is king while remaining on the throne ourselves doesn't work. It creates stress. It robs us of joy. It leaves us restless rather than peaceful. It is exhausting, deflating, and discouraging.

And you know it is.

This means my greatest challenge is to convince you that you are the reason you aren't happy. I'll do my best, but dethroning yourself is difficult in a selfie culture. You're not going to find much support from others, including other church members. We have built an entire kingdom on the belief that we are better kings than King Jesus.

In spite of this, and as counterintuitive as it may seem, crowning Jesus king of your life is the most thrilling, rewarding, and amazing thing you will ever do. If you will die to yourself and crown him your king, you'll experience real kingdom power, truth that works, and amazing, deep beauty in all you do. Crown him king, and all your relationships will change. Your feelings and emotions will change. Your hurts, habits, and hang-ups will find the power of healing. You will experience miracles. You will find peace. Joy. Purpose. Adventure. And when you die—as all of us will—you will die with a smile on your face. And you will be raised from death victorious. Forever.

Let's open the book of King Jesus, the sacred Scriptures, and discover who the real king is. When we do, we will also discover just how wonderful it can be when we stop our journey, get off the throne, and ask the king to take us on his journey. What a ride that can be!

The story of the Bible is this: Jesus of Nazareth has become the king of the universe.

The imperative of the Bible is this: we are to respond to King Jesus with faithful faith, which demonstrates itself in obedience-based discipleship.

And so this book has two objectives.

First, I want to show that Jesus is the king of the universe. We'll look at six biblical descriptions of King Jesus—six stages of revelation, if you will, about his divine kingship. We'll try to get a clear image of the king as well as of the kingdom of God he brings. As part of this process, we'll also look at fuzzy images of King Jesus, each of which sells him short. Fuzzy images dishonor Jesus. But they also rob us of the power, the truth, and the beauty he offers. We'll describe five fuzzy images and offer a brief critique of each.

Second, I want to show that we are to respond to King Jesus in faithful faith. There are various ways to describe what faith in King Jesus looks like, but I'm choosing the term "obedience-based discipleship" because I believe it most closely aligns with Jesus' call in the gospel presentation of the kingdom of God. Jesus expects us to put faith in him, and when we do this, we will become obedient to him. He is, after all, king of the universe. You don't merely believe in kings. You obey them.

To help identify key elements of obedience-based discipleship, I have chosen to build my argument on the final command of King Jesus in the gospel of Matthew, because Matthew's gospel is about how Jesus of Nazareth became king of the universe.

Here's Jesus' final command: "All authority in heaven and on earth has been given to me. Therefore go and make disciples of all nations, baptizing them in the name of the Father and of the Son and of the Holy Spirit, and teaching them to obey everything I have commanded you. And surely I am with you always, to the very end of the age" (Matt. 28:18–20).

There are five key elements in this program for obedience-based discipleship. Here they are, in the order of their appearance in Matthew 28:18–20.

1. Surrender to the authority of King Jesus.
2. Embrace the mission of King Jesus.
3. Immerse yourself in the life of King Jesus.
4. Obey the teachings of King Jesus.
5. Behold the presence of King Jesus.

If you embrace the elements of this program, you will discover a life truly worth living. It is a life full of power. Of peace. Of purpose, beauty, truth, and love. And it is an eternal life.

When my daughter was nine years old, I took her with me on a business trip to Los Angeles. It was her first time there, and she wanted to see everything. Because she is always a delightful human being, I was happy to oblige.

One hot afternoon, we went to Hollywood's Chinese Theatre, because everyone has to go there at some point in their lives. The only movie available to our schedule that day was John Hancock's *The Alamo*. I don't think Rachel had ever seen a PG movie before; I know she had never seen a PG-13 movie. She informed me that it was "illegal" (her word) for her to go to a PG-13 movie. But we had to go. It is Hollywood's Chinese Theatre. "Besides," I explained, "the rating probably only means there are a few bad words." So we entered. Her face was wild-eyed at the thought of getting away with something so illegal as watching a PG-13 movie.

We got popcorn and a drink. Always the cheapskate, I decided to get only one drink that we could share, a massive sixty-four-ounce cola. I asked Rachel to carry the popcorn bucket so I could carry the cola. But for reasons still unknown to me, she insisted that she was old enough to carry the cola, which was in a cup the size of a dumpster. The cup was sweating. Her hands were small. We argued. I tried to convince her she would drop it, but she played the "You don't trust me" card. So I relented.

You have already guessed the end of this story.

Going into the now-pitch-black theater straight out of LA's blinding sunlight, Rachel stumbled as she got into her seat. All sixty-four ounces of frigid cola spilled on the head of the guy sitting in front of us. It was a full baptism coming, as it were, straight from the heavens.

I cannot repeat what the poor man said, but I can assure you that it was far worse than any bad words we heard in our PG-13 movie. It might even have been illegal.

Rachel apologized, first to him, then to me.

"I should have trusted you, Dad."

Probably so.

And you should trust King Jesus. He is a far better king than you'll ever be. You will enjoy the full blessings of his kingship only if you do trust him by submitting to him in obedient discipleship. With you in charge, life is going to spill. It's only a matter of time. But if you allow King Jesus to transform your desires, you will find deep peace, true joy, and a real purpose.

You get only one shot at life. And life is too important for you to remain in control. How much better it would be if you let the designer of life, the lord of life, and the redeemer of life take over the controls!

To this day, whenever Rachel and I hit a bad spot, we sometimes laughingly say to each other, "Remember *The Alamo*." And whenever you hit any spot in life, you should say to yourself, "Jesus is king." He gets to decide what is right and what is wrong. He gets to decide how the universe will be played out. He holds your destiny in his hand.

And one day King Jesus is going to return. When he does, every knee will bow before him. One day he will confirm, once and for all, that he has all authority. Wouldn't you be better off if you handed it over to him now? Paul says that "at the name of Jesus every knee should bow, in heaven and on earth and under the earth, and every tongue acknowledge that Jesus Christ is Lord, to the glory of God the Father" (Phil. 2:10–11). He's already king. All you have to do is to give your life over to him.

Let's start now.

CHAPTER 2

JESUS CHRIST, KING OF THE UNIVERSE

Who is he, this King of glory? The LORD
Almighty—he is the King of glory.

—PSALM 24:10

There's a wonderful phenomenon that occurs when musicians get it exactly right.

It's called a "ringing chord."

The ringing chord occurs when the harmonics of several voices combine with each other to create a new frequency that sounds like additional voices. The ringing chord requires the right notes, and the overtones must be fairly strong. Above all, every voice must be pitch-perfect, and the whole must be in seamless harmony. It is fairly easy to explain mathematically, but that does not diminish its beauty. And if done well, it is truly beautiful: the ringing chord can make four voices sound like a roomful of musicians. It will send shivers down your spine.

We've all experienced similar phenomena—things that equal far more than the sum of their parts. There is nothing in oxygen or hydrogen that would predict that, when combined, they would create ocean waves, waterfalls, and coffee.

There is certainly no way to look at the lump of matter we call a brain and predict that it would produce the human mind, complete with its ethical, aesthetic, rational, and speculative capacities.

In the same way, every element of the gospel has its beauty, but when all the elements are combined in just the right way, the universe rings out in full chorus. "The sun lifts up his glorious voice, and moon and stars reply; all in one concert sweet, one lofty strain combine!"[2]

I've already mentioned that the story of the Bible is how Jesus of Nazareth became king of the universe, and the imperative of the Bible is that we must respond to King Jesus with faithful and obedient discipleship.

But for a variety of reasons, many of us have listened to only snippets and parts of the story of the Bible, so we have missed the ringing chord effect—the life-giving beauty, truth, and power of the whole and complete story. We have settled for what I will call "fuzzy Jesuses" in the next chapter. These are narrow slivers or even distortions of the story of Jesus that prevent us from hearing the fullness of who he is and therefore the fullness of how we should respond to him.

So we must start by retelling the story of how Jesus of Nazareth became king of the universe. This is the only story we have. And it is the only story that saves.

When you get all the notes of the story of King Jesus in complete harmony, you'll feel the room vibrate with power. Getting the whole story will change everything for you.

So who is King Jesus?

1. KING JESUS IS THE GOD OF THE UNIVERSE

In the opening chapter of the New Testament, the book of Matthew tells us that Jesus is to be called "Immanuel." It is a Hebrew term that means "God with us." This is important, for it tells us that the story of King Jesus starts long before creation. The story of King Jesus is a divine story; it is the story of God with us. Though the Bible is sometimes oblique about it, over and over again it teaches us that King Jesus is none other than "God with us" (Matt. 1:23).

It is essential that we start the story of King Jesus before creation, for he is none other than the God of the universe. As John says, "In the beginning was the Word, and the Word was with God, and the Word was God. He was with God in the beginning. Through him all things were made; without him nothing was made that has been made" (John 1:1–3). John settles the identity of Jesus (who is "the Word" of John 1; see v. 14). Jesus is the creator of all things; he is God himself. Paul puts it this way: "The Son is the image of the invisible God, the firstborn over all creation. For in him all things were created: things in heaven and on earth, visible and invisible, whether thrones or powers or rulers or authorities; all things have been created through him and for him" (Col. 1:15–16).[3] Jesus appeared in the form of a human, but he is one with God the Father.

The early church summed up the relationship between the Father, Son, and Spirit in a simple confession: there is one God in three persons—the Father, the Son, and the Holy Spirit. And the church summed up the nature of King Jesus in this confession: Jesus is fully human and fully divine. These two confessions (the Nicene and Chalcedonian Creeds), though not formulated in such language in the Bible itself, accurately capture the starting point of the story of Jesus. He is none other than the God of the universe—a member of the Trinity who became human (without diminishing his divinity) in order to redeem all of humanity. He created you. He created everything that is created. He will be king, because he already is king.

This matters not only because it is true (and truth matters!) but because if we fail to see that Jesus is divine, we will lose all his power. Jesus will change your life, but not by modeling good techniques, management principles, or activism. He changes lives by rescuing us from our techniques and management principles. With his divine power, he himself will transform you into the likeness of God when all your efforts have failed. Because he is God.

A friend of mine once followed King Jesus as the divine Son of God, but then he began to listen only to the podcasts of those who downplay or even deny the deity of Jesus. At the same time, my friend was going through major disappointments in life. Eventually my friend came to believe that Jesus was only a role model for social change and not the actual Son of God. Denying Jesus' deity, however, left my friend with no power, for people's hearts cannot really be changed without divine power. The more my friend tried to confront the world with his social views, the more powerless he felt, and the more powerless he felt, the more cynical he grew. He soon became a bitter, angry, and depressed person. The last time we talked, he told me that he doesn't believe in God anymore.

This is the devastating consequence of failing to understand that King Jesus is none other than the God of the Bible—the God who alone possesses the power to change the world. If you undermine the divinity of Jesus, you will lose his power. Jesus not only teaches us to love the unlovely; he empowers us to do so. And he empowers us to do so with great joy, not rage and resentment. His power can transform both the lives of the unlovely and the lives of those who love them.

The Jesus who is king is not just a role model; he is the God who will change everything if you trust and follow him. "Apart from me you can do nothing," King Jesus explains (John 15:5). Without Jesus as your God, you are on your own. That's a scary place to be in this broken world.

Consider another friend of mine. He grew up in a tough home, where he felt abandoned and abused. He eventually joined the marine corps and fought in Iraq. But the demons of his life piled up with every turn. Eventually he fell victim to several debilitating addictions that almost cost him his family as well as his life.

He joined a twelve-step program and soon found deliverance. The first three steps have become the theme song of his now-redeemed life: he admitted he was powerless over his life, that his life had become unmanageable, and that only a power greater than himself could restore him to sanity. "I made a decision," he told me, "to turn my will and my life over to the care of God—Jesus Christ, the Son of God." My friend now lives a fantastic life with a healthy family. He has led many, many others out of bondage through the power of the Son of God, King Jesus. But he could live such a life only because he plugged into the power of King Jesus as the very Son of God.

Whatever your struggles, King Jesus can resolve them, but not because he is merely a good role model, social reformer, or theologian. King Jesus can resolve them because he is God himself, bringing the very power of God into our lives to effect the changes that we require.

Get this right before you move on to any other angle of the King Jesus story, or you'll end up wasting a whole lot of effort trying to fix what you cannot fix. And you'll end up with a sad and lonely existence. You were made for communion with God, and if Jesus is not divine, he is only a massive distraction from life. But if you find the real Jesus, the divine Son of God, you'll discover divine communion. You'll find your purpose. You'll find hope. And you'll find his power.

2. KING JESUS IS THE HOPE OF ISRAEL

God in three persons created us so he could have communion with us. This is the most beautiful part of the garden of Eden story—not that we were at peace with the animals or possessed primal innocence but that God himself walked among us "in the cool of the day" (Gen. 3:8). God created us for the same reason many of us have children: God wants someone to love.

But we disrupted that communion when we sinned. God banished us from his presence because his holiness will not allow him to dwell in the middle of our unholiness. We were expelled from the garden. We were left in a creation broken by our own sin. And in case you think it unfair that we should live in a broken creation because of what Adam and Eve did, I remind you that every single one of us has thrown garbage into the water from which we must all drink. "All have sinned and fall short of the glory of God," the apostle Paul explains (Rom. 3:23). It is not that God doesn't want to hear us or that he doesn't love us. No, as the prophet Isaiah says, "Your iniquities have separated you from your God; your sins have hidden his face from you, so that he will not hear" (Isa. 59:2).

But God was not done with us. Far from it. The fall of humanity and the subsequent tarnishing of creation formed the starting point for a grand rescue effort. God would redeem his creation by restoring his rule among humans. And he would do this first through one man, Abraham.

It's a long, long story that comprises three-fourths of the Bible—the story of Abraham's nation, Israel. But for our purposes, it is important to realize two things.

First, we must realize that Israel and its Old Testament are not mere sideshows in the story of King Jesus. These form integral chapters in his story. God's dealings with Abraham and Israel form the first revelations of what it should look like when people submit to the kingship of Jesus. All of the Old Testament points to Jesus—his ethics, his holiness, his hope, his mission—who is the perfect embodiment of Israel and its Scripture.

This doesn't mean that we are still bound by the law of the Old Testament. The New Testament makes it very clear that nobody will be justified by keeping the law (Rom. 3:20). But it does mean that the Old Testament belongs to us Christians, and its truths are our truths. You don't want to unhitch yourself from the Old Testament, for in it we learn the first principles about how to live faithful to God. In it we get the opening statements about how to love God and others. The Old Testament was written so we could understand what the kingdom of God is. "Everything that was written in the past was written to teach us, so that through the endurance taught in the Scriptures and the encouragement they provide we might have hope" (Rom. 15:4).

The second thing we must realize from Abraham and Israel is that Jesus *is* the God of the Old Testament.

We should not think that Jesus is just any god. He is not. He is none other than the God of Abraham, Isaac, and Jacob. He is the God of creation. The God of the flood. The God of Moses and the Ten Commandments. The God of the judges, of David, of the Divided Kingdom, the exile, and the return. He is the God of the Hebrew prophets, the God of the Jewish festivals, and the God of the hope of Israel. The Gospels go to great lengths to demonstrate that King Jesus fills full (which is what *fulfill* means) the whole Old Testament. Jesus is none other than the God of Israel. He is the God Who Is, as he introduced himself to Moses at the burning bush: "I AM WHO I AM. This is what you are to say to the Israelites: 'I AM has sent me to you'" (Ex. 3:14). That's who King Jesus is.

What other God would Jesus be?

So . . . what do you get if you play a country song backward?

You get your wife back, your house back, and your dog back.

Maybe that joke isn't very funny, but it's a useful metaphor. What do you get if you reread the Old Testament seeing Jesus as the fulfillment of every single page? You get your God back, you get your people back, and you get your hope back. And you get your kingdom back. For the kingdom of God that Jesus came to announce was the exact same kingdom that the Old Testament prophesied and foreshadowed. We don't get to fill the term "kingdom of God" with our own utopic definitions. No, if we want to understand what the kingdom of God is, we must listen to the definitions the Old Testament gives us.

So while the New Testament emphasizes that Jesus is the fullest revelation of God and that he opens the kingdom of God to all the nations, we must learn what the Old Testament says about God and the kingdom or we will fail to understand Jesus as God and the kingdom he brings. Without the Old Testament, we will fail to see that Jesus is the same God who took sin and salvation seriously, the same God who delivered people from bondage, the same God who promises a redemption of all creation, the same God who makes covenants with his people, punishes evildoers, and saves those who turn to him. Jesus is *that* God, and his kingdom is *that* kingdom.

Here are just a few descriptions of the God who Jesus is: "The LORD, the LORD, the compassionate and gracious God, slow to anger, abounding in love and faithfulness, maintaining love to thousands, and forgiving wickedness, rebellion and sin. Yet he does not leave the guilty unpunished" (Ex. 34:6–7). These are powerful descriptions of the Jesus who wants to shepherd you. He wants to show you mercy. He loves being gracious to you. He is slow to anger; he abounds in love. He forgives us our sins. This is no mere Gandhi or Martin Luther King Jr. (as important as these men were). This is a God who wants a real, life-changing relationship with you!

But we also get our people back when we see that Jesus is the God of the Old Testament. God chose Abraham's descendants and formed a covenant with them. They were to be his people, receiving his truths and his power. Now, in King Jesus, we get to be grafted into that people. We all get to be Israelites. We get the truths God taught Israel. We get her mission. We get her promises, her hopes, her redemption, and her destiny. By seeing Jesus as the God of Israel, we enter a covenant with God—not exactly the old covenant but a new one modeled after the old, though far, far superior to it. We are no longer Jews by physical circumcision or by following a law. Now we get to be Jews by having our hearts circumcised and having our lives filled with the Holy Spirit. As Paul says, "A person is not a Jew who is one only outwardly, nor is circumcision merely outward and physical. No, a person is a Jew who is one inwardly; and circumcision is circumcision of the heart, by the Spirit, not by the written code" (Rom. 2:28–29). And now we get every promise God made to Israel about restoring lost humanity's place. We get these promises in our lives.

On a shelf in my home office sits a bottle of wine I bought a couple years ago in Israel. The wine was produced at a vineyard called Shiloh Vineyards, situated in the hills of Samaria. I stopped there on a visit to the West Bank because of something said in Jeremiah 31.

For more than two thousand years, there had not been successful vineyards in the hills of Samaria; all had been destroyed by invading armies. But in the last several decades, the wine again has begun to flow in the mountains of Samaria. I bought the wine—which I never intend to drink—as a reminder that God is faithful to his promises. For now, as a member of the people of God, I get to claim the promises of the Old Testament for a restored creation. I get the promises made to Israel through Jeremiah:

> Again you will take up your timbrels
>> and go out to dance with the joyful.
> *Again you will plant vineyards*
>> *on the hills of Samaria;*
> the farmers will plant them
>> and enjoy their fruit. . . .
>
> They will rejoice in the bounty of the Lord—
> the grain, the new wine and the olive oil,
>> the young of the flocks and herds.
> They will be like a well-watered garden,
>> and they will sorrow no more.
> Then young women will dance and be glad,
>> young men and old as well.
> I will turn their mourning into gladness;
>> I will give them comfort and joy instead of sorrow.
>> —JEREMIAH 31:4–5, 12–13, EMPHASIS ADDED

My bottle of wine is a constant reminder that King Jesus is the God of the Old Testament who is at work buying back every square inch of lost creation for his pleasure and for our good. When we understand that King Jesus is the embodiment of the God of Israel, all the promises of the restoration of Israel become promises made to us. In King Jesus, God is filling full the Old Testament announcement that he would one day redeem creation and bring it back to him in full and sweet communion. This God—King Jesus—will bring you home dancing and shouting for joy.

3. KING JESUS IS THE EMBODIMENT OF THE KINGDOM OF GOD

Now the story intensifies. Jesus came to bring to earth the will of God as it is in heaven.

For many of us, King Jesus has been reduced to a mere forgiver of sins. I certainly don't want to diminish the forgiveness of sins; without such, we cannot enter into communion with God. But this is just one facet of the big, hairy, audacious thing that Jesus came to do. For King Jesus came not merely to forgive sins or to take us to heaven when we die. He came to restore fully the reign of God among humans so that we could live in full communion with him both here and in the hereafter.

This means that with the coming of Jesus, God has done nothing short of announcing that the fulfillment of all the claims and promises in the Old Testament are present in Jesus himself. Jesus is the king, and his mission is to reestablish God's reign on earth as it is in heaven. This is why in the Lord's Prayer, Jesus prays his intent: "Your kingdom come, your will be done, on earth as it is in heaven" (Matt. 6:10). Jesus is not simply praying that we will acknowledge our sin and ask for forgiveness. He is praying that God's kingdom will begin to thrive here and now. On earth. Among us. Jesus is praying both that we will be saved and that we'll become part of the grand redemption of all of creation that God is determined to accomplish.

I love many of the older hymns that I grew up singing. I even love some of the gospel-song-era music that inspired my mama—with her beautiful voice—to make music before the king. But I have noticed how many of these songs relegate the work of King Jesus to the future: "I have a mansion just over the hilltop"; "I'm on my way to that fair land"; "When we all get to heaven." It's odd because the Bible hardly speaks of *going to* heaven at all.

Jesus didn't come merely to save us from our sins so we could go somewhere called heaven at the end of time. He certainly didn't come so we could sit on a cloud forever in an eternal church service. (Does the word "heaven" come to *your* mind when you think of an eternal church service?)

King Jesus came, in his oft-repeated words, to bring about the kingdom of God here and now. So while we need to understand that Jesus forgives sin and that we will get a fantastic hereafter, these are merely notes of the much grander, richer, and more beautiful song of God's redemptive plan for creation. King Jesus came not just to save us for heaven in the future. He came to transform us into citizens of the coming paradise here and now. Right now we get to begin lifting up the poor, as they'll be lifted up when King Jesus returns. Right now we get to speak truth to one another, as truth will be the language of the resurrection. Right now we get to live in peace with others, as we look forward to the peaceable kingdom. Right now we get to dance with joy, as joy defines the Spirit of God's kingdom. Right now we get to live where love reigns supreme, as nothing unloving will be allowed into the consummated kingdom.

Of course, such living is both counterintuitive and unpragmatic. After all, we are still foreigners and pilgrims in the world as it is (1 Peter 2:11–12). As it is, this world is not our home. But that doesn't mean that we abandon this world. It means that we adopt the mission God gave Israel: instead of abandoning the world, we live right smack in the middle of the world as citizens of a different world—the kingdom of God. We live differently from the world, but we do so for the sake of the world. We get the mission that God originally gave to Israel: we get to serve as witnesses to the world of another kingdom. "It is too small a thing for you to be my servant to restore the tribes of Jacob and bring back those of Israel

I have kept. I will also make you a light for the Gentiles, that my salvation may reach to the ends of the earth" (Isa. 49:6).

In the ministry of Jesus, we are taught how to live right now in the kingdom of God. We are shown how to conduct ourselves right here as we will one day live in the hereafter. In his very life, Jesus brings the reign of God to us so we can begin living now as it will be when he consummates it with a resurrected creation—a new heaven and a new earth (2 Peter 3:13).

4. KING JESUS IS THE CROWNED CONQUEROR OF SIN AND FUTILITY

Jesus was announced as the King of Kings at his birth and lived his life as the unacknowledged king of Israel. But his coronation did not occur until the crucifixion.

His killers meant it for evil. But in history's greatest twist of fate, the cross of Jesus served as the moment of his coronation. It was not an accident that Jesus was given a crown when he was crucified. And it is especially telling that Pilate directed that an inscription be placed on Jesus' cross above his head: "THIS IS JESUS, THE KING OF THE JEWS" (Matt. 27:37).

At the cross, Jesus completed the task for which he was sent to earth. In his life, King Jesus showed us how to begin living right now in God's kingdom. And in his death, Jesus offered us the atonement necessary to enter that kingdom. Jesus paid the penalty for our sin so that we could commune with a holy God. If we are to get the full story of Jesus, we will affirm the biblical doctrine of the atonement. Jesus came to bring the reign of God among humans, but he died so that we could gain the rightness necessary to live in God's kingdom. This is the meaning of the word atonement: in Jesus, God took upon himself the punishment for our sins so that we could stand in rightness before God. The atonement preserves God's justice—sins are punished, a necessary condition for justice. But the atonement also displays God's mercy—rather than punishing us, God takes upon himself our punishment. In King Jesus, God paid everything for us to be right.

But there is more. By dying, King Jesus "disarmed the powers and authorities" and "made a public spectacle of them, triumphing over them by the cross" (Col. 2:15). Satan had planned to keep us separated from God through the bondage of our sins. But Jesus' death set us free from our bondage, releasing us from all the hurts, all the evil, all the enslavement, and all the darkness Satan had intended for us. When the sun was darkened at the cross, the clock began ticking on the inexorable demise of everything that stands between us and God. In this way, Jesus' death on the cross became the one moment in all of God's redemptive history when King Jesus put on his crown. At the cross, Satan's fate was sealed. Life with God was made possible again, and the future of the kingdom of God was secured.

This is critical for understanding King Jesus. He is not a remote God who remains uninvolved in our lives. Nor is he a mere activist who dies a tragic death. King Jesus is the God who, in his justice and mercy, takes upon himself our penalty to prove that he is a just king, while at the same time extending unbounded mercy. He is the king who triumphs over all the forces of darkness that have stood against us.

This part of the story is very personal, for it means that King Jesus deals with my shame, my guilt, my brokenness, and my enslavement by entering my world and bearing my penalty upon himself. Because he bore my penalty, I am set free from all that has me broken. This is true even though I sometimes continue to act broken. I've been set free, but it may take me years to begin to act free.

I have struggled with anxiety most of my life. I don't know why. Is it genetic? Is it a lack of trust? Is it just the energy that I use to push myself harder? Whatever the cause of the anxiety, here is what I know about King Jesus. He has set me free from the bondage of anxiety. Because he became king, I have no reason to worry about the future; my king holds the entire future in his hands. He is going to work out everything for my good (Rom. 8:28).

Sadly, this hasn't stopped me from having bouts of anxiety. But when I allow myself to be anxious, it is not because I am anxiety's slave. What do I have to fear? As Jesus says, "See how the flowers of the field grow. They do not labor or spin.

Yet I tell you that not even Solomon in all his splendor was dressed like one of these" (Matt. 6:28–29). No, now when I allow myself to indulge in anxiety, it is because I find anxiety to be an old friend. Jesus has set me free, but I haven't completely stopped hanging out with my old friends. I've been set free from my bondage, but it's taking time for me to live consistent with my King Jesus freedom.

The cross of Christ is a sad witness to our humanity, but it is a thrilling statement about God's mercy. God, in King Jesus, sets me free from bondage! Once and for all, he declares that this broken creation has been bought back by God, and he himself bears the cost. In the death of King Jesus, the redemption I crave is fully offered, not through my denying sin's existence (which never, ever works) but through my declaring it powerless over me. The cross of Jesus becomes the crowning moment of Jesus' life. It becomes the open door through which I can enter again into sweet, sweet communion with the God who made me and loves me to no end.

5. KING JESUS IS THE ENTHRONED RULER OF THE UNIVERSE

When Jesus was raised from the dead, he ascended into heaven, where he took his seat at the right hand of the throne of God. If the cross of Jesus affirmed his coronation, the resurrection and ascension of Jesus serves as the moment of his enthronement. As the resurrected Jesus says, "I was victorious and sat down with my Father on his throne" (Rev. 3:21).

At the resurrection, Jesus declared all other powers to be empty. Rome had no power over him. Sin has no power over him. Satan has no power over him. Even death has no power over him. There is not a power, authority, or principality anywhere in the universe that has authority over Jesus. In the resurrection and ascension, as Paul says in his hymn, "God exalted him to the highest place and gave him the name that is above every name" (Phil. 2:9).

This is the message that launched the Christian movement. Jesus Christ, who died for our sins, has been raised from the dead and now rules the universe from the throne of God!

Standing on the slopes of Zion, from which the kings of Israel had long ruled, the apostle Peter put it this way: "This man was handed over to you by God's deliberate plan and foreknowledge; and you, with the help of wicked men, put him to death by nailing him to the cross. But God raised him from the dead, freeing him from the agony of death. . . . Therefore let all Israel be assured of this: God has made this Jesus, whom you crucified, both Lord and Messiah" (Acts 2:23–24, 36).

It was the power of the resurrected Jesus that sent the disciples into all the nations to preach the kingdom of God. Had Jesus remained in the grave, there would be no victorious king to preach. Had Jesus not ascended into heaven, he would not be reigning today. But he did not remain in the grave, and he did ascend into heaven, where he took his place on the throne next to the Father.

This is fantastic news, for it means that King Jesus currently sits on the throne of God, ruling over creation. We are not to think that this world is unfolding randomly or beyond the lordship of King Jesus. It is not. We can walk in full trust because we know that Jesus is now sitting at the right hand of God's throne. You don't have to wonder who is in charge. King Jesus is. And you can trust him.

And one more thing: the resurrection of King Jesus points to your future. You too will be raised from this dead life to walk in a resurrected creation, a creation that looks a lot like the paradise we lost, but only much, much better. Because King Jesus was raised from the dead, you now have a future.

6. KING JESUS IS THE RETURNING KING OF VICTORY

All this means that we currently live between the inauguration of the kingdom of God and its final consummation. We inhabit the land of in-between. It's an ironic life. The kingdom of God has already come, but it is only a small seed at this point—as King Jesus says, it starts as a mustard seed before it can overshadow the whole garden (Mark 4:31–32). It will not be consummated until King Jesus returns. But even here and now we are to live as though the future consummation has already occurred. This can be hard. Right now the world is run by imposters, frauds, and rebels. We live in a world, as Paul says, inhabited by "the ruler of the kingdom of the air, the spirit who is now at work in those who are disobedient" (Eph. 2:2). But right smack in the middle of this kingdom of darkness, we are to live as children of light. We live in a despotic and tyrannical world, but we are expected to demonstrate the culture of the holy, gracious, and peaceful kingdom about to come. We truly are, as Peter says, "foreigners and exiles" (1 Peter 2:11).

But we shouldn't find misery in this irony. It is a beautiful irony. For we get to taste, here and now, a rich sampling of the fruits of the coming kingdom.

In the Greco-Roman world, it was not uncommon for an important general, dignitary, or even emperor to make a visit to a city. Their coming was marked by festivals, parades, and envoys going out to meet them. They often came with a great army and the display of immense glory. They would bestow great favors on the city, occasionally building some monumental edifice for the city's inhabitants. Sometimes as a show of their justice, they would punish those who had been bad. And they would reward those who had been loyal to them.

The return of Jesus is very much like the coming of an emperor.

King Jesus will come with an army of angels, with the trumpet call of God, with the voice of the archangel, and with the final day of judgment (1 Thess. 4:16). He will build a new city. When King Jesus returns, he will bring an end to all other kingdoms and vanquish all challengers to his authority.

He describes his return in various ways. Sometimes he uses apocalyptic language: "The sun will be darkened, and the moon will not give its light; the stars will fall from the sky, and the heavenly bodies will be shaken" (Matt. 24:29). Sometimes he uses the language of judgment or shepherding: "All the nations will be gathered before him, and he will separate the people one from another as a shepherd separates the sheep from the goats. He will put the sheep on his right and the goats on his left" (Matt. 25:32–33). Sometimes he speaks of his second coming as a feast: "I say to you that many will come from the east and the west, and will take their places at the feast with Abraham, Isaac and Jacob in the kingdom of heaven" (Matt. 8:11). And he speaks of it in comforting terms: "Do not let your hearts be troubled. You believe in God; believe also in me. My Father's house has many rooms; if that were not so, would I have told you that I am going there to prepare a place for you? And if I go and prepare a place for you, I will come back and take you to be with me that you also may be where I am" (John 14:1–3).

The rest of the New Testament uses similar language to describe the second coming of Jesus: as an apocalyptic end, a judgment, a feast, a comfort, and more.

However it's described, the simple and profound truth is that we now live in anticipation of the return of our king. The story of the Bible is how Jesus of Nazareth became king of the universe. The imperative of the Bible is that we live faithfully to King Jesus here and now, in anticipation of that return. We get to show the world here and now what paradise is going to look like when Jesus returns. We get to inhabit the land of in-between.

And what a paradise it will be. John describes it in Revelation 21–22 as a city whose streets are paved with gold. It is called the New Jerusalem, and the city will stretch hundreds of miles. Its entrance will be marked by gates made of pearl, and the apostles' names will be inscribed on them. There will be no need for a sun, for King Jesus himself will be our light. There will be no need for a temple, for God himself will live among us. There will be no more suffering. There will be no more sin. There will be no more pain, no death, and no dying. "I am making everything new!" the enthroned king declares (Rev. 21:5).

THE JOY OF IN-BETWEEN

In 1942, during World War II, the Japanese Imperial forces captured Burma from the British. At that point, it seemed that the Axis forces of Japan, Italy, and Germany might well take over half the world. Things looked grim.

Thousands of British soldiers were taken prisoner by the Japanese and herded into horrific POW camps. Many of them were murdered: shot, beheaded, crucified, or tortured to death. The sufferings many endured were indescribable. Those who were not executed often died slow and painful deaths from disease, brutal treatment, and starvation. Nobody who went into those camps came out the same.

But somewhere toward the latter half of the Japanese occupation of Burma, a bright English prisoner found a way to construct a radio. It was risky: were the radio to be discovered, he and others would be killed. Building the radio took an astonishing degree of resourcefulness. They used tinfoil from a tea box they found. For resistors, they rubbed tree bark on a string. They improvised a power source, headphones, and everything else needed. After months of trial and error, they secretly built a functioning radio.

From where they were imprisoned, the POWs had no idea how the war was going. For all they knew, England had ceased to exist and its soldiers would all die in this camp—until they listened to their new radio. They picked up a BBC broadcast coming out of China. Everybody was amazed.

Everything changed when they heard their first broadcast, even though it didn't announce the end of the war. The broadcast didn't mention the war at all. For thirty minutes they heard about the crop yield of English farms that season. That's it. Then the battery died.

But that thirty-minute broadcast changed everything.

If the British were talking about crop yields, not only did England still exist, but the news of the war was evidently so good that the BBC could afford to talk about hops and wheat. It was all the POWs needed to hear. They immediately recognized the thrilling reality: we are going to win!

From that day forward, the lives of the POWs were never the same. The men were filled with confidence. The end of the war was approaching. They were still in between—living between the initial victories of the war and its final consummation. But knowing that the end was coming was all they needed.

They smiled, some for the first time. They began to show each other uncommon love and grace. They even treated their guards with kindness: one POW struck up a friendship with a Japanese guard that lasted for sixty-four years after the war.[4] After all, they would soon be going home. They had heard it from the best source on the planet—the BBC. They had heard it in the language of their hearts—English. In a crazy world of pain and grief, they had heard that a new normal awaited them.

One radio broadcast about their future didn't liberate these soldiers from the POW camp, but it did set their hearts free. They could survive the in-between because they knew what was coming.

King Jesus came into a world in rebellion against God and announced the arrival of God's kingdom. He was crowned on the cross and raised to sit on the throne of God. It started small, but it's not going to end that way. Soon King Jesus will return and bring with him the fullness of the kingdom in complete victory. Every wrong will be made right. Goodness, beauty, and truth will reign. All pain, every sickness, and even death will be vanquished. God himself will live among us. Everything shall be made new.

Doesn't knowing this change everything for you? Soon you'll be home. Soon you'll be free. Soon you will be with the God who made you and wants to redeem you. As Paul promises, "Listen, I tell you a mystery: We will not all sleep, but we will all be changed—in a flash, in the twinkling of an eye, at the last trumpet. For the trumpet will sound, the dead will be raised imperishable, and we will be changed. . . . Thanks be to God! He gives us the victory through our Lord Jesus Christ" (1 Cor. 15:51–52, 57).

But we don't have to wait until the consummation to live under the rule of King Jesus. We cannot afford to wait until his return. He teaches us to begin living here and now under his rule. Right now we can show the love that characterizes the kingdom. Right now we can speak truth and mercy to a world full of hurt. Right now we can care for the poor, release the enslaved, and proclaim the Lord's favor. Right now we can join the mission of Jesus to make disciples of all nations. And right now we can do all these things and more in the power that he offers us through his Holy Spirit. Right now.

Sure, the fullness of the kingdom has not arrived just yet. But it has already started with the coronation of King Jesus. We can, we should, we must, live in his kingdom here and now. Jesus is already king. In what other kingdom could we possibly serve?

Getting the whole King Jesus story right will fill the room with joy, with power, with music. The sum of his story is greater than its parts. Jesus is more than a good man, more than the forgiver of sins, more than a social activist. He is the King of Kings and the Lord of Lords who sets you free. He is the bringer of the kingdom of God, which has already started and into which you are already invited. And soon he will be the one who returns in final victory to establish, once and for all, the reign of God among all of creation. *This* is who King Jesus is.

He is none other than the king of the universe.

CHAPTER 3

THE CHALLENGE
OF FUZZY JESUS

"Who is this?"

—MARK 4:41

An older member of my church died a year ago. Well, I say older. He was ninety-six years old when he died. He had been quiet and reserved for as long as I had known him, and I really had no idea how important he had been. Until his funeral.

It turns out my friend, a man by the name of Glenn Snoddy, had patented a device that started a revolution in the music industry.

Snoddy had just returned from World War II, in which he had been an army electronics specialist. He moved to Nashville just as the music industry was beginning to bud. Because of his electronics background, he landed a job as a sound mixer in the studios of Nashville. Soon he was engineering the music of such stars as Patsy Cline and Johnny Cash.

The invention happened by accident.

He was on the team that was recording the song "Don't Worry" by Marty Robbins. Suddenly a tube malfunctioned in the console through which the guitar was routed. The guitar sound immediately turned out fuzzy and reverberant. The engineers continued recording, planning to fix the problem in a second recording. But Robbins and the producer listened to the sound. It was funky. No one had ever used that sound before. They decided that though it risked the success of the recording, they would produce the song with the fuzzy sound in it.

The song was a hit. Suddenly everybody wanted that sound in their recordings. Snoddy quickly built a device to recreate the sound—the fuzz box. And the rest is history. If you've ever heard the opening fuzzy guitar to the Rolling Stones song

"(I Can't Get No) Satisfaction," thank my friend Glenn Snoddy, whose fuzz box deliberately distorted the sounds of musical instruments in wildly successful ways.

Unfortunately, many of us have created our own fuzz boxes that distort the real King Jesus to make him sound suspiciously like us.

We must be honest here. Most of us want a Jesus who affirms our values and interests. We want a Jesus who makes us feel good, helps us get what we want, and advances our causes. So we are tempted to pick and choose only select parts of the story of Jesus to create a Jesus who looks like us.

We have just surveyed the only story that the Bible wants to tell: the story of how Jesus became king of the universe. It is a power-filled, honest, and beautiful story. But it demands that we, in the words of King Jesus, die to ourselves, take up a cross, and follow him (Luke 9:23). Because many of us don't want to die to ourselves, we tend to distort Jesus to make him look like us. We pass him through a fuzz box.

Because this is such a serious problem, I have devoted this chapter to describing some of the fuzz boxes through which North Americans tend to pass King Jesus. As you read these descriptions, I ask you to consider whether you want the Jesus who really exists—with all his truth, beauty, and power—or are settling for a distorted Jesus.

THE HOLIDAY FUZZ BOX

Many of us like having some version of Jesus around. Humans are born with a spiritual predisposition, so we are happy to find some sort of religion. Religion can be studied as a branch of anthropology. To be *Homo sapiens* is to be in some sense religious. North Americans gravitate toward Jesus because for North Americans, Jesus still represents some sort of religion. Appealing to Jesus makes us feel spiritual.

What many don't want, however, is a Jesus who makes demands of us. We prefer a Jesus who is just here to help us be happy and get what we want. We prefer cultural Christianity to the kingdom of God.

And so, many of us construct a fuzz box that I'm calling the holiday fuzz box. With this fuzz box, Jesus becomes more like Santa Claus: he's still timeless, generous, and from up north, but the Holiday Jesus doesn't make many demands of us. His main job is to give us things we want. He prefers that we be nice, not naughty. But in the end, he is going to give us stuff even if we are not that nice. He is just a big, nice guy who wants to help everybody get the life they want.

Tom and Amy have Jesus plugged into a holiday fuzz box. They have been members of my church for years. Or, to be precise, they have been members of every church I've ever served since my first day of ministry. I've known hundreds of Toms and Amys.

Tom and Amy have an okay marriage, but it will never be great. They are too self-centered to have a great marriage. They raised their children in church, but both of their kids quit going shortly after they went off to college. It was never as important to any of them as were sports, school, and success.

I don't want to judge Tom and Amy, but I've lived with them enough to know that they prefer the distorted Holiday Jesus to the clear, full symphony of King Jesus. They can pray to Holiday Jesus, but they don't have to. Like Santa, this Jesus wants them to be good, but he winks when they, as one author said of herself, drink a little, cuss a little, and party a little. After all, he's sometimes serious, but he's not that serious. Holiday Jesus applauds when Tom and Amy volunteer to serve at the homeless shelter, but his main goal is to help them become successful—in their relationships, in their careers, and in getting what they want out of life. He expects them to be polite, respectable, and happy. But he doesn't ask for boldness, sacrifice, or holiness. It's a good thing too, because they aren't about to offer such faith. They are too busy becoming everything they want to be.

And if things in Tom and Amy's life fall apart, they can pretty easily stop believing in Holiday Jesus, because they never really took him seriously in the first place.

Years ago, Ron Sider prophetically pointed out about such cultural Christians that "by their daily activity, most 'Christians' regularly commit treason. With their mouths they claim that Jesus is Lord, but with their actions they demonstrate allegiance to money, sex, and self-fulfillment."[5] Jesus puts it even more bluntly: "I know your deeds, that you are neither cold nor hot. I wish you were either one or the other! So, because you are lukewarm—neither hot nor cold—I am about to spit you out of my mouth. You say, 'I am rich; I have acquired wealth and do not need a thing.' But you do not realize that you are wretched, pitiful, poor, blind and naked" (Rev. 3:15–17).

The holiday fuzz box presents a Jesus who affirms nice, suburban lives that never really swore allegiance to King Jesus. There are vast numbers of cultural Christians in North America, but that large number is collapsing quickly. If Jesus is nothing other than a nice guy in the sky, then when the going gets tough, other nice things distract us, or when the church finds itself out of step with the values of its surroundings, cultural Christians just drop out. And that's what they're doing all over the place: dropping out. This is very bad news for cultural Christians, and we mourn the loss of those who are abandoning the faith. Nonetheless, this may strengthen the church, since having a large number of uncommitted members dumbs down everybody's faith.

The sad thing is that cultural Christianity, with its Holiday Jesus, has robbed some of you of the thrill that could have been yours in King Jesus. Early followers of Jesus made radical sacrifices, surrendering every corner of their lives to Jesus. They took enormous risks, but such risks gave them enormous rewards. They saw terrorists become Christian missionaries. They experienced divine healings. They built schools, orphanages, and hospitals. They saw demons run like rats. Eventually they even saw the emperor of Rome bow his knee before King Jesus.

But such rewards came only when they submitted every area of life to the king: their speech, their careers, their sexual desires, their hearts, their minds, even their children. Some were so radical they lost their lives. But with each martyr who fell, a dozen more people were convicted to follow Jesus. "The blood of martyrs," said one of them, "is the seed of the church."[6] Half-hearted, cultural Christianity cannot produce full-throttled, earth-shattering results. The second chapter of the book of Acts describes a shock-and-awe church full of miracles and power. But if you want to experience Acts 2 miracles, you have to make Acts 2 commitments.

One day, millions will grow up and realize that Holiday Jesus doesn't exist.

THE TRANSACTIONAL FUZZ BOX

Many evangelicals have created a truncating, limiting fuzz box for King Jesus that narrowly focuses on salvation, by which they mean "going to heaven when I die." Evangelicals typically do this by hearing only Paul and the book of Romans. Don't get me wrong. Romans is one of the most beautiful books ever written. It discusses our most fundamental need: the need to be right with God (called "righteousness" in most translations, although I prefer the simpler term "rightness"). The Roman church was divided between Jews who followed the Torah and Gentiles who didn't. At stake in the church at Rome was a simple question: Are we made right with God through the Torah plus Jesus, or are we made right through faith in Jesus plus nothing? Paul answers unambiguously: Rightness is found in Christ alone. Christ plus nothing equals everything.[7]

Romans is a true book, a powerful book, an honest book, and a fully inspired book. But it's not the Bible's only book.

The focus on Romans since the days of Martin Luther has sometimes led us to miss the full music of the gospel. Like reducing a beautiful corpus of music to a few simple singsongs, a focus only on the question of rightness may give us a partial picture of King Jesus, but it doesn't give us the whole picture. Jesus came to bring the reign of God in its totality; he came to change everything. He did not come simply to forgive me of my sins, as important as this is. So while Romans answers a very narrow question—How can I be right before God?—the rest of the Bible answers an even larger question: Who is Jesus, and what did he come to do?

Beverly learned to use the transactional fuzz box, but millions of others have used it too.

In the neighborhood I lived in as a boy, there lived two women somewhat older than I was. Back then we neighborhood boys lived outdoors; Snoddy's fuzz box had been invented, but video games had not. So every day we roamed the streets, playing football, hanging out with neighbors, and otherwise looking for something to do.

These two women who lived in the neighborhood were not good women. Without going into detail, it was claimed by some of the neighborhood boys that one could go to their house and have illicit relations with the women.

One day before I fully understood this about them, however, I was sitting on their front porch with a group of friends. Suddenly a couple of church people came walking up. They had been knocking on doors and challenging people to invite Jesus into their hearts. They seemed happy to have so many of us gathered in one place there on the front porch.

The two door knockers told us that Jesus had died for our sins. They told us that Jesus loved each of us and wanted to save us from the guilt of our sins. In this they were right. But then they explained to us that all we had to do to be saved was to say the sinner's prayer. You know how it goes: admit you are a sinner and ask Jesus into your heart. Most of us said the prayer, including Beverly.

"What else should we do?" Beverly asked.

"That's all," one of the witnesses answered.

"Nothing else?"

"Well, you should go to church and live a good life, but you are now saved whatever else you do. Once Jesus saves you, you can never be lost."

Beverly thanked them. They left. She immediately invited some of the boys into the house "to play." I left and never returned.

Even at the age of ten or eleven, I knew that this formulation of the gospel was wrong—terribly wrong. To teach people that all they have to do is recite some recipe—a recipe not even found in the Bible!—and they will forever have a secure place in heaven is to warp the gospel of King Jesus. I understand that these witnesses were trying to be faithful to the principle of salvation by faith alone. And I honor them for having the courage to knock on doors, something I myself have done thousands of times. But these witnesses never called for biblical faith, which includes penitent allegiance. They merely offered a transaction. Say this formula, and you will get salvation. The formula is a far, far cry from the way that Jesus made disciples.

Jesus doesn't call us just to make a brief transaction and then return to our pagan lives. He calls us to deny ourselves, take up a cross, and follow him (Luke 9:23).

If you have allowed yourself to believe that making a simple transaction is the same as kingdom living, you have missed the message of the Bible. Don't get me wrong. There is a transaction that occurs in the life of a believer as he or she passes from what the Bible calls the kingdom of darkness into the kingdom of light (Col. 1:12–13). But this is not the full story of the Bible. Instead the message of the Bible is that God has come among us in the person of King Jesus to establish his kingdom, and he invites us to die to ourselves and live in submission to him from this point forward, not just to make a simple transaction and then move along. Faith is how we enter that kingdom, but if upon entering the kingdom, we immediately replace King Jesus with King Me, we never really believed him in the first place. Biblical faith is more like allegiance than mental agreement.

Jesus came to change the entire creation. He came to set us free from bondage. He came to show us how to love. He came to teach us a new way of life. He came to give a redemptive purpose to everything we do—our work, our relationships, our politics, our art, and even our music.

The transactional fuzz box condenses the gospel of the kingdom of God into a few short affirmations. And those who listen only to this fuzz box will have empty, un-Jesus-like lives.

THE TRADITIONAL FUZZ BOX

Some Christians have seen through the emptiness of the holiday and transactional fuzz boxes. They've been baptized, become active members in our churches, avoided many of the vices that plague our world, and proclaimed a high view of the Bible. But instead of following a powerful and living Jesus, these believers have defined themselves by a long list of dead traditions.

For these believers, traditions about worship, church governance, and morality have eclipsed the greater matters of the kingdom, such as justice and mercy. Large numbers of traditionalist believers were on the wrong side of the civil rights movement, often justifying their despicable behavior by appealing to the very Scriptures they sought to uphold. Some have fallen for the prosperity gospel, twisting King Jesus' message into a strategy for getting rich in this life. And running through the twentieth-century history of such believers has been a harsh thread of judgment that, at least for many people, obscured the love of God behind a dark cloud of terror. Hell seemed more important than heaven.

These Christians plug Jesus into what I'm calling the traditional fuzz box. The music of this box is hyperjudgmental, unchanging, and at times downright scary. It includes songs about getting right with God, about sin and error, and about the coming judgment. There is little to celebrate in the music coming through this fuzz box. The traditional fuzz box is built in response to the fear that somebody, somewhere, may be happy.

I don't want to be misunderstood here. There are many traditions that are lovely and healthy. Think of the many beautiful and enriching traditions we have about Christmas. But traditionalism is not merely the observation of traditions. Traditionalism replaces biblical teaching and the power of Jesus with archaic and artificial rules and regulations that are often used to marginalize and punish others and that often ignore the beauty of the kingdom of God. Traditionalism occurs, Jesus says, whenever "you nullify the word of God" by what you have handed down (Mark 7:13).

Ben and Cathy play Jesus through the traditional fuzz box.

They were raised faithfully going to church three times per week. Their parents were strict; strictness made sense to their parents, whose lives had been shaped by the Great Depression. But it morphed into traditionalism for Ben and Cathy. By the time I got to know them, their view of the Christian faith was rigid, judgmental, and harsh. Several of their children had rebelled against their faith and had left the faith altogether. The children who stayed in the church turned out argumentative and restless.

I have butted heads with the Bens and Cathys of the church for years, and most of those years they have seemed angry with me. They are out of sorts that I don't wear a necktie when I preach. They don't like hearing loud, contemporary music, kneeling during prayer, or clapping after baptisms. They don't like people who are different from them, and they distrust the other churches in town. More than anything, they hate change, and they are unable to keep that hatred to themselves.

Many Bens and Cathys have reduced the grand story of God's redemption of the entire creation to a few arguments over such things as what kind of music we have in church. I once preached at a church in the Northeast that had just gotten over a major disruption. When I asked the pastor what had been the problem, he explained that he had moved the piano from the left side of the stage to the right side. "Some of our members wept before they left us for good," he explained. I could only shake my head.

The emphasis on getting doctrine right often blinds Ben and Cathy to the weightier matters of justice and mercy. One time while I was at Ben and Cathy's church as a visiting teacher, an obviously poor man visited the church. After the service, he came up to Ben and me and asked us if we would be able to help him get some food for his family. I know that people often take advantage of the church's generosity. I've been taken advantage of hundreds of times. But Ben's response still haunts me. Looking with disgust at the man, he shook his head. Then he looked the poor man in the eyes and said, "Don't come back here."

As people are endlessly taught to focus on the rules rather than on King Jesus, many leave the faith because of the misfocus of the traditional fuzz box. The harsh, rigid, hyperjudgmental Christians who insist on the minuscule points of doctrine have forced many believers to look for alternative forms of Christianity. How many young people have abandoned biblical Christianity because the only people they heard speak of it did so in traditionalist, harsh, and unloving ways? How many of you have been wounded by the needless shame produced in such condemning environments?

And how many of you listen to King Jesus through the distortions of the traditional fuzz box? Do you fret endlessly over how people dress at church? Over what kind of music we have? Over who gets to be in charge, how ugly lost people are, and sermons on grace in which sinners are welcomed to the table of the king? When I was an older teenager, my minister preached a sermon on grace. In it he described a loving king who was willing to set aside numerous traditions for the purpose of including the lost in his kingdom. A subscriber to the traditional fuzz box met him in the foyer and—right in front of my eyes—threatened to break his jaw if he ever preached on grace again.

The heart of the gospel of King Jesus is love, not hatred. Not anger. Not "our way." The gospel is *good* news, not bad news. King Jesus came to bring about the will of God on earth as it is in heaven. He did not come to create a holy club where only a few traditionalists get to be saved from the unwashed heathen.

If songs are distorted by the traditional fuzz box, we won't hear the good news. And one day, those who listen through this fuzz box—those who fuss and fight with each other all the time—are going to eat each other alive. One day there will be no traditional fuzz boxes left.

THE NEW AGE FUZZ BOX

Some people have abandoned biblical Christianity because the only examples they've seen of it are, as mentioned before, the poor examples provided by hyperjudgmental Christians. But some have abandoned the apostolic witness of Scripture because they don't like its demands for rightness and holiness. They want a form of spirituality, but they don't want to be bound by the clear teachings of the Bible to live righteous and holy lives.

These Christians have fallen for something of a Zen Jesus; they listen only through a New Age fuzz box.

For the New Age Jesus, what matters most is feeling good about yourself, living an authentic life, and being inclusive of everyone. If the Jesus heard through the traditional fuzz box is hyperjudgmental and old-fashioned, the Jesus of the New Age fuzz box is hyperinclusive, trendy, and suspicious of truth. Listeners to the New Age fuzz box are generally universalists. They believe that God is in everyone, and all you have to do is look deep inside and find him. Sin may exist in the New Age fuzz box, but it's really nothing more than a weakness or a failure. Therapy rather than repentance is the cure. For New Age Jesus, salvation is enlightenment, which one gets through contemplation and self-discovery. New Age Jesus hardly needs the Jesus of history, since New Age Jesus' message is more a therapy and less a matter of historical fact. This is why the New Age fuzz box downplays Scripture or searches for trajectories out of Scripture or claims to have grown beyond the Bible.

The New Age fuzz box offers soothing tones that make for great Zen moments, liquid massages, sentiment, and cushy books. It offers inspirational sayings about the goodness of all people. And it teaches us to find ourselves by looking inward rather than by looking upward.

As with the other fuzz boxes, I don't want to be misunderstood here. Jesus does offer healing (Mal. 4:2). He offers inward peace, deep joy, and the discovery of who we are by accepting what he says about us. Meditation is a great gift from God, and love is the most fundamental mark of the kingdom. But that's not what the New Age fuzz box presents. The New Age fuzz box replaces biblical healing, biblical joy, biblical peace, and biblical self-reflection with New Agey concepts drawn from pop psychology, other religions, and self-inspired sentiment. It is such a distortion of the faith that Jesus becomes unnecessary.

Darren listens exclusively to the New Age fuzz box. He grew up in an evangelical church, but when he went away to university, he developed doubts about his faith. It started when his brother announced that he was gay. Darren could not bring himself to believe that his brother, whom he deeply loved, was wrong. Darren had been having sex with his girlfriend for years, compromising the tenets of his own faith. *Maybe,* he began to think, *who you have sex with doesn't matter to God at all.*

Soon Darren found himself listening to the podcasts of several popular progressive thinkers. He heard that the Bible mentions same-sex activity only a handful of times and that such texts have been misunderstood by the whole of Christianity, for all time, and all over the world until only the last few years, when progressive thinkers in North America discovered a new meaning to the faith. We should stop obsessing about sex and focus instead on human goodness, one progressive pointedly concluded. Further, believing in sin produces shame, and shame is our biggest enemy. Darren heard that Jesus' love is inclusive and that Jesus would never exclude or shame anyone. In short time the subtext of progressivism began to make sense to him: We humans are not sinners in need of salvation at all. We are basically good, not basically sinful; all we need is a better focus on the flow of God that runs through every one of us. We need to dismiss anything that makes us feel shame.

To make this therapeutic message work, the New Age fuzz box has to undermine the Bible, which doesn't support its claims. No problem. The New Age fuzz box sentimentalizes the Bible, asserting that the Holy Scriptures are simply the reflections of other spiritual seekers collected to help us find our own spirituality. Our job, Darren soon came to believe, is to measure the Bible by our own sentiments. Those parts that disagree with us should be dismissed. We get to decide what is authentic and what is not, depending on how we feel.

But the New Age Jesus is vastly different from the Jesus who is king. At the end of the day, the New Age fuzz box is nothing other than a reflection of upper-middle-class and wealthy Western elites. Progressivism is an expression of American Protestant liberalism, historically the religion of white elites.[8] And dismissing shame doesn't make it go away. It simply pressurizes shame; suppressed shame will eventually burst forth in a hundred other ways.

Early in my ministry, I counseled a woman who had grown up in an abusive family. Her mistreatment included sexual abuse. By the time she became a teenager, she had learned that offering her body for sex would get her lots of male attention, which she confused for love. Soon she had developed a deep sense of shame, guilt, and self-loathing. Of course, much of her shame was the result of other people's "sexual freedom"; she was a victim of shame more than a perpetrator. But her feelings of shame were present nonetheless. Several counseled her that the shame wasn't real; she should simply push it away. But the more she denied the shame, the more it debilitated her.

Listening to the real Jesus, she learned that shame is a spiritual reality, not merely a psychological one. She knew that there was a real spiritual war going on for her soul. This was not simply a matter of therapy. It was a cosmic battle for her life.

I encouraged her to resist the temptation to suppress or deny the shame, but rather to confess it to Jesus, asking him to remove it. After all, he had rebuked demons and driven them out of a thousand other people through the years, including me. Maybe he would drive out this demon too. She quit denying the shame. She quit trying to manage it. She quit pretending it wasn't there. Instead she laid out her pain before King Jesus. She asked an older woman to pray with her, which the woman did for several weeks. The victim asked Jesus to remove the shame.

Several months later she told me that though she still had baggage she knew might take years to overcome, the shame was gone, not because she denied its existence but because King Jesus saved her from it. Hers became a wonderful story of a woman set free. King Jesus—the Jesus who really is—has the power to destroy the bondage of our sins. And he broke her bondage to shame. Last I heard, she had gotten married and was living a life set free by the real Jesus—King Jesus, the Jesus of Scripture.

So which would you prefer: trying to persuade yourself that the shame you feel is not there, or living a life in which the bondage of shame has been forever broken?

If you want access to the loving power of King Jesus to break your bondage, you must first realize that the bondage is real. The New Age fuzz box denies the true nature of our diseases. But the real Jesus cures them.

This is why so many across the Global South—the region stretching from Africa to Southeast Asia—are coming to the kingdom of God through a strict loyalty to the Bible. They open the book, obey it, and find themselves released from their bondage. In the place of their bondage, they find peace, joy, and love. It's only in the decadent West, where we don't want the Bible to be true, that people devote enormous amounts of time trying to replace the Scriptures with their own sentiment. So we remain in bondage.

The New Age Jesus is the product of Western self-inspired sentimentalism. The day will come when our current sentiments will fade, proving that sentimentalism never offered a place to stand in the first place.

THE PROTEST FUZZ BOX

The Christian faith is not just designed for personal salvation. Jesus came to change the world, not just to save souls. So history has been deeply shaped by the Christian faith. We Christians have established hospitals, built cities, saved babies, cared for widows, started schools and universities, invented alphabets and written languages, led in the arts and sciences, developed legal theory, invented the concept of human rights, and a whole lot more. Christianity has always had a social conscience, because the kingdom of God reaches every corner of the planet. And Christians have changed the world because we believe that we can change the world, one person at a time.

The protest fuzz box distorts this world-changing work of the kingdom. The protest fuzz box is not about building a better world by changing hearts. It is not music for the peaceful, humble servant for the sake of the world, such as King Jesus modeled. It is not really about building a better world at all. It is about a rage against the world as it is. It distorts the story of the kingdom through numerous rants and shouts and screams about what is wrong with the world. The music in this fuzz box won't build a single city. It won't save an abandoned child, start a university, care for a widow, or take the good news to a lost world. The protest fuzz box offers a steady stream of angry music for people who see everything as identity politics, and it affirms their resentment about such things as race, sex, gender, class, and politics.

Let's be clear. You will hear the Scriptures speak often of such matters as justice, mercy, and care for the poor and marginalized. And anyone who follows

Jesus will work for these virtues—both in private relationships and in public venues. Nonetheless, the Scriptures place these values in the context of individual Christian lives that have first taken seriously personal holiness and personal rightness in Jesus Christ alone. So though you will hear of justice and mercy in the Bible, you won't hear the protest fuzz box there. If you want to listen to Protest Jesus, you must follow him on Twitter, read his angry blogs, and listen to his subversive podcasts. The protest fuzz box is something like a Che Jesus—a Jesus who feels ethical when yelling at others and overthrowing institutions.

Natalie is a devoted listener to the protest fuzz box.

Like Darren, Natalie grew up in evangelical churches. But by high school she had grown angry at the church. Natalie began to think that the leaders of her church, most of whom were old men, were both chauvinistic and backward (she may have been right). The more she thought about church, the angrier she became. Eventually her inner rage grew into a deeply held cynicism. At first she expressed her doubts about God altogether. But at some point she discovered the writings of young Christian social activists. She was hooked.

In the protest fuzz box, Natalie found affirmation of her anger and resentment. The music screamed subversion—rage against imperialism, authority, whiteness, the rich, cisgenderism, homophobia, male privilege, immigration laws, and a whole lot more. Social justice *is* the kingdom of God for Natalie, and political correctness is its language.

So Natalie follows MSNBC religiously. She tweets social causes multiple times per day. She joined the Women's March, wearing a pink p***y hat. She loathes Wall Street and longs for a socialist government, which she thinks is outlined in the Sermon on the Mount. She favors laws that would punish Christians for refusing to do such things as cater same-sex weddings. She hates Israel but refuses to criticize Islam, considering it an oppressed religion.

Natalie has no use for orthodoxy, historic Christianity, or the apostolic witness. She doesn't waste much time thinking about the end of time. She isn't concerned about such things as holiness. Nor is she interested in personal salvation—broken people can be fixed if we repair broken social systems. So for Natalie, Christianity is little more than a rage-fueled social and political program designed to bring about a utopia here in this life.

But Natalie has misread Scripture (if she read it at all). King Jesus is concerned with such matters as social structures and politics, but he goes about redeeming these in the opposite way. He offers to change the hearts of the individuals who make up these systems, through his redeeming love. When enough people are saved, the systems will greatly improve. This is how the Christian faith has changed the world throughout history.

So King Jesus' way is the way of service, humility, gentleness, and love. King Jesus understands that holiness gives us healthy boundaries, transforming our lives and restoring broken systems. And King Jesus knows that things won't fully be restored until he comes again, bringing with him the consummation of all things—a new heaven and a new earth.

The protest fuzz box does not produce the peace, the joy, and the thrill that King Jesus offers. It produces manic, frustrated lives. The gentle way of King Jesus leads with love, with understanding, with grace. If you are constantly posting online rants about politics and culture, do you really think you're representing King Jesus? How many rants against Caesar did Jesus tweet? If you want to follow Jesus, you should start on your knees. You should be firm in your convictions, but civil in your life. You should serve as Jesus served, become humble as he was humble, and love as he loved. The most thrilling response to King Jesus is not self-assertion. It is self-surrender. Surrendering to King Jesus is how we find peace, not fighting political and cultural wars.

Natalie doesn't realize it, but the destruction she is unleashing with Protest Jesus will one day turn on her. For in the end it is love, not rage, that wins.

SURPRISED BY THE JESUS WHO IS

In April of 2009 a very, very ordinary woman strutted out on a stage. She was forty-five years old, and her hair was, shall we say, not in style. Her eyebrows were bushy. She was a bit overweight. She had a thick Scottish accent. Her father was a miner, her mother a shorthand typist. Bullied as a child, she was told that she has Asperger's syndrome, a form of autism. She was so ordinary that the audience snickered at her. People rolled their eyes.

But here she was, contestant 43212 on the English television program *Britain's Got Talent*. To the giggles of the audience, she said that she hoped to become "as successful as Elaine Paige."

After interacting a brief moment with the judges, she burst forth with a song.

Yes, I'm talking about Susan Boyle. Boyle's performance that night may have been the most notable moment in the entire history of reality television. She sang the song "I Dreamed a Dream" from the play *Les Misérables*, and the crowd screamed with delight. Her act was world-class. No one had ever seen such an amazing performance from such an unlikely person.

Boyle has gone on to become a Grammy-winning superstar musician. She has sold millions of recordings. She has topped the *Billboard* charts multiple times. She has met prime ministers, celebrities, and even the queen. She is now a million-aire. And to top it all off, at the end of 2009 she appeared on her own television special, singing a duet with Elaine Paige.

But nobody saw it coming. The audience was looking for someone younger. They were looking for glamor. They were looking for someone who looked like them.

But Boyle broke out of the people's expectations and became a sensation.

The world wants a Jesus who looks like them. Some want a Holiday Jesus who expects little from them but offers them a nice Christmas Eve program. Some want a Transactional Jesus who comes into their hearts when they offer a prayer but then allows them to live as pagans. Some want a Traditional Jesus who makes them feel smug in their rightness. Others want a New Age Jesus who aligns with their ever-changing sentiments. And some want a Protest Jesus who sides with them in their rage against pretty much everybody else.

But none of these Jesuses are real. All are inventions of the imagination, designed to give people what they want. Imaginary Jesuses don't satisfy. They are no more real than unicorns.

The real Jesus, however, not only satisfies but empowers, elevates, heals, guides, and restores. The real Jesus can set you free from your bondage.

Are you struggling with depression? The Traditionalist Jesus will just depress you more, but King Jesus can heal you of your disease. I know this, because he has done this very thing for me.

Are you concerned about the poor? The Protest Jesus might be able to join you in screaming at capitalism, but King Jesus can provide you with the resources to serve the poor. I know this, because he has provided me and my church with—I'm not making this up—millions of dollars for the poor. Every week, we celebrate the joy of serving the poor here and around the world with the resources that our king has given us.

Are you struggling with temptation? The Transactional Jesus will just tell you to forget it; you were forever fine when you said the sinner's prayer. But King Jesus—the Jesus who is—will break the bondage of your temptations and remove their power. He will set you free. He's done it for me and for hundreds of my friends.

Given what the real Jesus can do, why in the world would you want to judge him by your own preferences? Nobody knew Susan Boyle would burst forth in a million-dollar song. But she has now become a legend. In the same way the audience dismissed her, the world rejected King Jesus. They crucified him. And every fuzz box that brackets out the Jesus who is for the Jesus we might prefer crucifies him again.

But King Jesus rose from the dead, and he invites you to join him in his resurrected kingdom. So throw away your old fuzz boxes and listen to the clear, full symphony of the king who is. Give it up for King Jesus!

CHAPTER 4

SURRENDER TO THE AUTHORITY OF KING JESUS

Jesus came to them and said, "All authority
in heaven and on earth has been given to me."

—MATTHEW 28:18

I have watched people die.

It goes with being a minister. You sometimes get invited to join a family at a hospital bed or in a hospice-arranged bedroom as a loved one takes his or her last breaths. It is usually calm and peaceful, though filled with emotions.

But sometimes it can be odd. I've known of dying people who saw the light. I've known of others who passed with odd smiles. I've also known of a few who went fighting. The mind does strange things as death arrives, releasing massive doses of chemicals, making odd electrical connections, and sometimes producing visions. People can say strange things when they're dying. And sometimes they are aware enough to choose their last words.

What would you say if you knew you were dying and you got to choose your last words?

One website has collected a number of last words of well-known people.[9] It's a bit morbid to read the site, but it is also instructive. According to this site, Winston Churchill's last words were, "I'm bored with it all." "Pistol" Pete Maravich collapsed during a basketball game. His last words were, "I feel great." John Wayne's last words, spoken in response to a question from his wife, were, "Of course I know who you are. You're my girl. I love you." And eerily, the last words of Apple founder Steve Jobs were, "Oh wow. Oh wow. Oh wow."

Last words can be fascinating because, at least when we get to pick them, they reveal what matters to us the most. The love of family. The accomplishments or failures of life. The impending arrival of eternity.

So here are some last words that are truly revealing: "All authority in heaven and on earth has been given to me. Therefore go and make disciples of all nations, baptizing them in the name of the Father and of the Son and of the Holy Spirit, and teaching them to obey everything I have commanded you. And surely I am with you always, to the very end of the age" (Matt. 28:18–20).

These are the very last words of Jesus in the gospel of Matthew. Since the gospel of Matthew is all about the question of how Jesus of Nazareth became king of the universe, its ending should be seen as a summary of everything Matthew has been presenting. Matthew 28:18–20 ought to be seen as the summary of the entire story of King Jesus and its necessary imperative: Jesus is now in possession of all authority because he alone has become king of the universe, and we are to respond to him by taking obedience-based discipleship into all the world.

What better summary of Matthew's gospel could there be? What better summary of Jesus' work could there be? What better summary of the mission of your life could there be?

I want to use Jesus' final words in the gospel of Matthew as a guide for the rest of this book. I want to show that the five statements of Jesus in these last words summarize how we are to live our lives. They demonstrate the proper response to the coronation of King Jesus. If you will make the final words of Jesus your first priority, you will have a thrilling, satisfying, and rich life. And when your last words are spoken, they too can be something like, "Oh wow!"

Here are the five statements, arranged as a strategy for following Jesus.

1. Surrender to the authority of King Jesus: "All authority in heaven and on earth has been given to me."
2. Embrace the mission of King Jesus: "Therefore go and make disciples of all nations . . ."
3. Immerse yourself in the life of King Jesus: ". . . baptizing them in the name of the Father and of the Son and of the Holy Spirit . . ."

4. Obey the teachings of King Jesus: ". . . and teaching them to obey everything I have commanded you."
5. Behold the presence of King Jesus: "And surely I am with you always, to the very end of the age."

The remainder of this book will take up each of these statements and show how faithfully responding to them will bring you a rich and satisfying life. I'll let these five statements define what I mean by our term "obedience-based discipleship."

Let's start with the first one: surrender to the authority of King Jesus.

WHO'S IN CHARGE?

The last words of King Jesus in Matthew's gospel begin with the assertion that all authority in heaven and on earth has been given to him. In the last twenty years, we have heard a lot more talk in North America about the kingdom of God. This is healthy, as such language had been somewhat hollow in evangelical circles. But if we are going to talk about the kingdom that Jesus brings, we must also talk about the authority that Jesus has. It will not do to talk about kingdom work if you don't submit to the authority of King Jesus. There is no kingdom where there is no king.

To be king is to exercise authority. This is a fundamental truth that must be embraced if we are to live in the kingdom. Jesus did not come to establish a democracy. The kingdom of God is not a republic. In the kingdom of God, you don't get a vote. Either you submit to the authority of your king, or you face the consequences that all insurrectionists, frauds, and rebels face. It's really that simple. And you really will make a choice.

Jesus is over all three branches of government: the legislative branch (he establishes the truth), the executive branch (he executes truth), and the judicial branch (he decides who is living consistent with the truth). Let's restore a robust view of the kingdom of God, yes. But to do this, we must also restore a robust view of the full authority of its king. We must acknowledge that if we live in the kingdom of God, we'll relinquish our authority and submit to his.

Notice how many ways the Gospels establish the authority of King Jesus.

He exercised authority over nature. "He got up, rebuked the wind and said to the waves, 'Quiet! Be still!' Then the wind died down and it was completely calm. . . . They were terrified and asked each other, 'Who is this? Even the wind and the waves obey him!'" (Mark 4:39, 41).

He exercised authority over sickness. "When Jesus had called the Twelve together, he gave them power and authority to drive out all demons and to cure diseases, and he sent them out to proclaim the kingdom of God and to heal the sick" (Luke 9:1–2).

He exercised authority over demons and the spiritual forces of evil. At the beginning of Mark's gospel, Jesus cast out a demon from a possessed man, and the crowds uttered in delight, "What is this? A new teaching—and with authority! He even gives orders to impure spirits and they obey him" (Mark 1:27).

He exercised authority over the religious leaders of the day. Repeatedly he proved them wrong, and repeatedly the people were astonished at his authority. "When Jesus had finished saying these things, the crowds were amazed at his teaching, because he taught as one who had authority, and not as their teachers of the law" (Matt. 7:28–29).

King Jesus has authority over prime ministers, presidents, and all other kings of this world. Standing before Caesar's own representative in his trial, Jesus explains to Pilate that "You would have no power over me if it were not given to you from above" (John 19:11).

So what is authority? It is the right to establish the rules, to command people to obey them, and to enforce them, rewarding and punishing accordingly. King Jesus has all of these rights. He establishes what is true; we do not. He has the right to expect our obedience; we don't have the right to negotiate his truths. And he will reward and punish according to our obedience to his rules.

But authority is a big problem for North Americans. We are endlessly conditioned to distrust authority. We have restaurants that tell us they have no rules. We buy bumper stickers that suggest that we should question authority. We see car ads that invite us to color outside the lines. We have movies titled *Breakin' All the Rules*. Women want bad boys for lovers; men want wild women. Even to children, Disney's Elsa sings, "To test the limits and break through. No right, no wrong, no rules for me. I'm free!"

Some of our distrust of authority is well deserved. With the rise of social media, we have learned that there are a lot of people and entire institutions that are, shall we say, challenged when it comes to moral authority. But much of the distrust of authority in North America is little more than an infantile desire to remain in charge. Americans want to command their own destiny, define their own existence, and determine their own rules, even when they don't know how. Even when it has devastating results.

We have commandeered a word for this, a word that once meant something good, but which for some has become an idol. It's a good word that is now misused by those who want to justify rebellion and self-centeredness. The word comes directly from a Greek term literally meaning "self-directed." We have been conditioned to think of it as a word of deep conviction, a word that will get you a welcomed spot on the talk shows. But sometimes it is a mere cover for propping up ourselves as puppet kings.

So what is this commonly used term for rebellion?

Authenticity.

I know that *authentic* can be a good word meaning something like "from the heart" or "sincere" or "real." Sometimes it is a good word. But does the term authenticity not often serve as a mere cover for rebellion?

I have a friend who asked me to visit with someone who had just moved into our area, whom we'll call Robert. Robert was once a minister, but he began to pass Jesus through the New Age fuzz box. As he did, he was taught to look deep inside himself rather than straight into the eyes of King Jesus. He was taught that Jesus' primary interest is our personal fulfillment. Looking inside for personal happiness, Robert soon left ministry and now says that he doesn't believe that

Jesus is the Son of God. Before I could make the visit, my friend contacted me and said, "Never mind that visit. Robert has now abandoned his wife and child and moved away to find what he is calling his authentic self." In this sentence, *authentic* doesn't mean "sincere" or "honest." It means "rebellious" and "self-centered."

Robert made an oath to love his wife "until death separates us." He swore that oath in front of two hundred witnesses, in a church, in front of a Bible, and, most significant, to his king. Now he has decided to ditch the oath he swore so he can make himself king. And he does so appealing to the comfortable word authentic. He wants us to believe that he has embarked on a noble search for the "real Robert." But what he really did was betray his king, kick him off the throne, and crown himself king. Jesus addresses this: "No one who puts a hand to the plow and looks back is fit for service in the kingdom of God" (Luke 9:62).

It's a terrible misuse of an otherwise good word. But it's also a terrible use of a life. Having Jesus as your king is not a burden or a form of enslavement. It certainly is not a form of inauthenticity. Jesus is no tyrant. He is a life-giving king, for he designed you, created you, and loves you even more than you love yourself. He knows what's best for you, and as he says, his burden is light and his yoke fits properly (Matt. 11:30).

The real burden of living occurs when we don't have a king who loves us. It is when we each appoint ourself as god that the world careens out of control. Anarchy may sound good on paper, but in real life it leads to destruction. This is why synonyms for anarchy include such terms as riot, mutiny, disorder, misrule, chaos, tumult, turmoil, mayhem, and pandemonium.

King Jesus doesn't exercise authority for his own good, and he is not a tyrant. He rules for our good, and the kingdom of God is the best kingdom in all of eternity. The authority of Jesus is not a burden. It is a blessing. King Jesus is a better king than we'll ever be.

Which brings me of course to LeBron James. LeBron James has a personal trainer.

James ranks among the greatest athletes in history, with multiple awards, championship games, and statistical achievements under his belt. His teammates call him King James. His net worth is near three hundred million dollars. Why? Because he may be the best basketball player who ever lived.

So why would King James want a personal coach?

Because even James knows that doing it his way brings limited success. James knows that he is successful because he has had great coaches. Without guidance, support, training, and firm rules, you would never have heard of LeBron James. James follows a leader. And because he submitted to someone else's lead, he is, well, King James.

In the same way, we require guidance, support, love, and divine power to flourish as humans. We are not designed to guide ourselves. We turn out to be very poor guides when left on our own. So the authority of King Jesus is not a bad thing; it is for our own good. It is the guidance we require to fully flourish. As Jesus says, "The words I have spoken to you—they are full of the Spirit and life" (John 6:63).

I once read a story of a sixty-seven-year-old woman in Europe who was traveling from her hometown of Hainaut Erquelinnes, Belgium.[10] She intended to pick up a friend at a train station in Brussels, ninety-three miles north of her home. Somehow her GPS got it wrong. Instead of traveling ninety-three miles to Brussels, she drove all the way to Zagreb, Croatia, a nine-hundred-mile journey that took her two days. You would think that at some point she would have realized the problem before ending up in Eastern Europe, nine hundred miles from home.

But her problem was that she followed the wrong guidance system—her GPS was off that day. Way off. In the same way, many of us are trusting our own navigation systems, designed by our own selfish hearts, and hoping we'll end up in paradise. But if you want the utopia that is the kingdom of God, you must accept the authority of the king who rules that kingdom.

I DID IT HIS WAY

Let's take a look at how submitting to the authority of King Jesus can enrich our lives in four categories of life: relationships, money, our bodies, and our emotions. In each case, we'll see that King Jesus is a better king than we'll ever be.

Relationships

Some time back I had a falling out with a friend. The details of the struggle are not important for my story, but let's just say that we were both very hurt and somewhat angry. I could hardly sleep, and when I did, I had nightmares. As the anxiety mounted, I began to feel a pressure on my chest. The pain lasted several days and became so great that I had my wife drive me to the ER for X-rays, thinking I was having a heart attack. I was relieved (sort of) when the cardiologist looked at the tests and said, "Good news. You only have anxiety."

I knew that I had to find a way to offer forgiveness and reconciliation to my friend. Dealing with the problem my way was causing all kinds of issues. So I called him up and asked to meet with him. I don't know what I expected, but I was surprised when we sat down.

"You are not my enemy, and I am not yours," he said right off the bat. "Instead we are both facing a challenge from the devil, who wants to divide us so he can hurt us both. I say you and I reconcile now and team up against the evil one instead."

It was a solution taken directly from the pages of King Jesus' playbook. "If you are offering your gift at the altar and there remember that your brother or sister has something against you, leave your gift there in front of the altar. First go and be reconciled to them; then come and offer your gift" (Matt. 5:23–24). Either of us could have handled our relationship in an ugly, self-serving way. We could have tried to hurt each other. We could have even taken our grievances on the road for the whole world to see. But because we offered up our relationship to the authority of King Jesus, it was saved. Our families were spared the agony of our bitterness. And my anxiety disappeared. Though my friend eventually moved to another city, even today when we see each other, we hug, smile, and know that King Jesus gave us a miracle.

When we acknowledge the authority of King Jesus over our relationships, we discover true love. We can find peace, even in difficult relationships. We can be set free from the crushing bondage of unforgiveness. We will find the path to becoming better, truer, and more loving husbands, wives, parents, children, and friends. Under the authority of King Jesus, our relationships will blossom into some of the most rewarding parts of our lives. We will find true love, for we will learn to love truly. That's because King Jesus is a better king than we'll ever be.

Money

Dave Ramsey has probably done more in North America to release people from financial bondage than a hundred college professors. His Financial Peace University class has set tens of thousands of people free from debt and exposed them to the opportunity to become, as he says, outrageously generous.

One reason Ramsey's plan works is because it is modeled, at least in part, after the teachings of the Scriptures of King Jesus. Work hard and ethically (Eccl. 9:10; Col. 3:23–24; 2 Thess. 3:10–12). Live within your means (Prov. 13:11; 1 Tim. 6:6–8). Be content with what you have (Phil. 4:11–13). Get out of debt (Prov. 22:7; Rom. 13:8). And be generous (Ps. 41:1–3; 2 Cor. 9:6–8).

We could easily forget that though King Jesus once said he didn't even have a pillow for his head, he owns everything. "The world is mine, and all that is in it," the Father says (Ps. 50:12). This means that King Jesus' plan for money is far, far better than ours will ever be, for he created money, loaned it to us, and knows its best use. With his plan, we find peace, joy, and flourishing.

Several years ago, my congregation went through a very difficult time, and I knew that we needed some sort of massive focus change to get our minds off our pain. I went away on a prayer retreat to ask God what we should do. By the time the retreat was over, I was convinced that we needed to a vision that would plunder the evil one's work and grab a victory out of our pain.

I returned, and after I spent time with my elders praying and strategizing about it, we asked the church to rally to a vision so huge that if it were ever accomplished, we would know it was by the power of God. The vision was for our congregation to stop doing church as usual and become part of the worldwide renewal that God is already doing. We would make disciple making the main thing. We would open a school for learning how to think like Christians.

We would pursue the goal of becoming a multiethnic church. We would host a television program to influence other churches to join the vision. We would commit to planting sixty thousand new churches. And we would become a house of prayer.

To launch the initiative, which we called our "2020 Vision," we would need to raise 1.6 million dollars. I didn't think we could do it, but we cast the vision, worked hard, prayed hard, faced down intense criticism, and targeted Easter Sunday of 2013 as our harvest Sunday.

When March 24, 2013, rolled around, I was crazy nervous. People generally give to buildings; everybody understands the need for a building. But I was asking people to give to something we couldn't show in blueprints. I was asking them to give to a dream.

I gathered in the room with several people who oversee our finances and the campaign leaders, and we began to count the pledges. We had already heard some amazing stories of giving. One young girl had made hundreds and hundreds of cookies, sold them, and given the money to the vision. An older woman donated a very expensive diamond ring, saying that it would be better used for the kingdom. Two families donated their wedding rings. People sold artwork, had yard sales and bake sales, sold stocks and bonds, and offered various services as donations. People gave property. One man promised a tenth of all the proceeds from a new job he was taking. A sixteen-year-old boy gave the money he had been saving for his first car. People young and old alike made financial commitments in amounts that stretched them, then doubled those amounts.

As the group counted, I paced the floor, praying. *Just give me 1.6 million dollars,* I prayed. Over and over.

When the count was over, the finance committee members looked at me and said, with joy in their eyes, "We didn't make 1.6 million dollars."

They said, "The total pledged is 6.1 million dollars."

We asked. He answered.

That's what King Jesus can do with money. After all, the cattle on a thousand hills belong to him (Ps. 50:10).

Our Bodies

King Jesus has authority over our bodies. That too is very good news.

Many are unaware of just how much the rise of a godless view of sexuality and gender in America has correlated to the rise of a thousand social ills we all hate. In the teaching of Jesus, sex is a gift given to humanity as a bond intended to join one man and one woman in a committed, married relationship for life. Jesus says that such a union is created by God himself (Matt. 19:1–9). Paul says it is nothing short of a mystical symbol of Christ's union with his people (Eph. 5:31–32). Sex outside of marriage is tantamount to a desecration of the temple of God, since our bodies are his temple (1 Cor. 6:19–20). Same-sex activity is a deviation from the gift God intended us to enjoy, and one that results from our fallenness as humans (Rom. 1:18–27).

When we fail to honor King Jesus' authority regarding sex and gender, we create a world of hurt for ourselves. I'm not arguing that sex is the most important matter in the Christian faith; it is not. But I am arguing that it is a load-bearing wall, and when we deny the authority of King Jesus in sexual and gender matters, we risk the collapse of the whole house. As America continues to make sex its central idol, we can expect to see more and more damage and decay around us.

Why is there such poverty in an otherwise superwealthy nation? Why are our incarceration rates through the roof? Why is the suicide rate climbing? Why the need for a #MeToo movement? Why so much mental illness? Why so many gangs? Why are there a million new cases of STIs every year? Why so much loneliness, abandonment, and hopelessness?

Every single one of these social diseases can be linked to America's failure to honor the sexual and gender ethics of King Jesus, for the collapse of the family often creates children with multiple emotional, economic, social, behavioral, and spiritual challenges.

Take just the example of fathers in North America abandoning their children, through either uncommitted sex or marital unfaithfulness. The massive number of fatherless children has increased the number of children with mental illness, depression, and unending anxiety and loneliness. Fatherlessness increases the likelihood of children growing up in poverty. It removes a critical role model from their lives, leaving them without the unique love of a father. As these children try to compensate for what only a stable home can provide, they act out in damaging ways, using illegal drugs, living rebelliously, and desperately spending their lives looking for hope. They too then enter commitmentless relationships, and the outbreak of social diseases continues. As one thirtysomething woman whose father left the family when she was young explained to me, "I'm forever painfully wondering what it is about me that made my dad not want me."

And this doesn't even account for the number of babies who are killed in abortions, as pregnant women find themselves feeling hopeless in the face of their sexual histories.

But it doesn't have to be this way. We could follow the ethics of King Jesus. I want you to imagine with me what the world would be like if everyone followed the sexual and gender ethics of King Jesus. Borrowing from an excellent blog by Sean McDowell, here is just one snapshot of what the world would look like if everyone submitted to the authority of King Jesus in matters of sex and gender.

> There would be no sexually transmitted diseases. No abortions. No brokenness from divorce. Every child would have a mother and a father and experience the love and acceptance each parent uniquely offers. There would be no rape, no sex abuse, no sex trafficking, pornography, and no need for a #MeToo campaign. There would be no sexual exploitation, no sexual abuse, no AIDS, chlamydia, herpes, HPV, or syphilis, no unwanted pregnancies, no pain from divorce, no deadbeat dads, no men who leave their wives for other women. No child would have to grow up in a home where a mom or dad merely abandoned them in order to "do it *my* way."[11]

As McDowell concludes, "Think of the healing and wholeness if people simply lived Jesus' life-giving words regarding human sexuality."[12]

I'm not arguing that biblical sexual ethics will make sense to a hedonistic North American culture. But I am arguing that Jesus' ethical system—including his sexual ethics—is by far the best in the world. We make a grave mistake when we believe that our way is better than the way of King Jesus. After all, his authority over everything is based on truth, power, and beauty. It is not capricious or self-serving. The ethics of King Jesus are offered to us because they are good for us. Doing it your way may feel good for a while, but if you want lasting truth, lasting power, and lasting beauty, you must submit to the ways of King Jesus. *All* authority in heaven and on earth has been given to him.

Our Emotions

King Jesus also has authority over our feelings and emotions. After all, he created us, and "in him we live and move and have our being" (Acts 17:28). This is a wonderful reality, for our feelings and emotions can become our greatest source of bondage. And King Jesus can rewire our hearts so that we choose positive emotions regardless of what we face.

A friend of mine does clandestine church planting and disciple making in the Middle East and in East Africa. He has brought thousands of people to King Jesus. Several months ago, he wept as he told me of the brutality these Christians often face in some Muslim-dominated areas. But he explained that while he was crying over their struggles, they were rejoicing that they got to share in the sufferings of Jesus. "They are the happiest people I've ever known," he explained. One woman, imprisoned for seven years in a partially buried, six-by-six metal container with only a hole in the top for air, food, and water, came out with a permanent glow on her face. "For seven years," she explained, "I walked in circles in the glory of God. I wish everyone could have what I now have." She felt its pain, but her emotional response was supreme joy.

Jesus can take the pain caused by a mother who never loved you or a father who abandoned you and use it to teach you to depend on his love alone. And he can lead you to a rich and satisfying ministry of loving others in crazy ways that people from stable families may never know. He can take the dread of cancer and show you the beauties of the world around you. "I'm glad I had cancer," a friend once told me. "Because now I see even the gorgeous detail of a single leaf in a way you, David, never will. Now every minute of my life matters." Jesus can take the feelings of abandonment that one experiences in a divorce and turn them into a mission to save marriages. One of my friends went through a painful divorce, but she has thrown herself into helping others manage the feelings of abandonment. "I'm not glad that I had a divorce," she said to me. "But I wouldn't trade my ministry for anything in the world now that I've gone through one."

All authority in heaven and on earth has been given to King Jesus, including the authority over our hearts. One of the most wonderful gifts King Jesus offers you is a new heart. It was promised long before his earthly ministry. "I will give you a new heart and put a new spirit in you; I will remove from you your heart of stone and give you a heart of flesh. And I will put my Spirit in you and move you to follow my decrees and be careful to keep my laws" (Ezek. 36:26–27).

I recently read of a man who lost the most precious thing he had on earth—his daughter. She died suddenly in an automobile accident. Because she was an organ donor, her heart was given to a man who was dying from heart failure. Eventually, through a program that offers donors and recipients the chance to meet, the man found out who had received his daughter's heart. To highlight the beauty of organ donation, he rode his bike fourteen hundred miles to meet the recipient of his daughter's heart.

When the father of the donor finally met the recipient of the new heart, they hugged and cried. Then the father pulled out a stethoscope and, with the blessing of the recipient, placed it against his chest. He heard again, for the first time in years, the very heartbeat of his daughter. Everyone cried.

When we submit our hearts to the authority of King Jesus, he offers to give us his heart, one that is no longer in bondage to broken, misery-producing, and lonely emotions. When God puts his stethoscope to our lives, he hears a heartbeat he recognizes.

THE JOY OF SURRENDER

So all authority in heaven and on earth has been given to King Jesus. And we will find true life when we submit to that authority.

How do we do this? Jesus himself gives us a summary answer: "Whoever wants to be my disciple must deny themselves and take up their cross daily and follow me. For whoever wants to save their life will lose it, but whoever loses their life for me will save it" (Luke 9:23–24). To submit to the authority of Jesus is to die to ourselves each day, but it is also to live for him each day. Every day, we bring him everything we are and allow him to shape it. Every day, we offer him our full allegiance. And every day, he changes us to become more like him.

It sounds frightening to give up control to King Jesus, but it leads to the most awesome of lives. A friend of mine who once served as an athletic director for a major university told me that he had learned something from his athletes. "You can have awesome, or you can have comfort. But you cannot have both." Many of us believe we will find comfortable lives when we keep ourselves in charge. But by doing so, we lose any opportunity for awesome. And we rarely find comfort on our own either. If you want an awesome life—a life filled with power, with truth, and with beauty—you have to choose to surrender to King Jesus in every area of your life. It may prove to be uncomfortable, especially at first, but it will definitely turn out to be awesome. For it is a wonderful thing to give over control to someone with more power, wisdom, and love than we can ever imagine.

I suppose this is why I like the few cruises that I have had the opportunity to take.

I'll never forget the first one. Julie and I took our two children on the Disney Cruise, which was, at least at that time, cheaper than a week at Disney World.

I had assumed that cruising would not be much fun. You are stuck on a ship, and someone else gets to make pretty much all your decisions—what and when you will eat, where you can go, and what you will do. But since much of my life has involved constant, intense, and pressurized decision making, it turns out I liked not having to make decisions. This ended up being one of the best vacations of my life for exactly that reason. No decisions! I didn't have to plan activities for the four of us; I didn't have to attend endless committee meetings; nobody cared what I wore. I didn't have to pick where to eat supper; all I had to do was decide between filet mignon and pan-fried trout.

Instead of making my own decisions, I trusted the cruise director. And not just any cruise director; remember, this was a Disney Cruise. Our cruise director knew everything that I would like and arranged the trip so my wife and children and I would have both comfort and awesome. Surrendering to the director of the happiest company on earth turned out to be one of those rare intersections between comfort and awesome.

King Jesus has become the cruise director for my life. He doesn't always offer me comfort and fun. King Jesus often calls me out of my comfort. But whenever I submit to his authority, I get awesome. I get to see the amazing things he is doing in the world.

Even in the short years since my church gave so sacrificially toward our 2020 Vision, we have seen dozens of miracles, hundreds and hundreds of baptisms, the planting of thirty new churches, and a whole lot more. We have discovered that there are many more movements out there, most of them far bigger than we are. Somehow we just found each other. And rich partnerships have grown from a simple decision to join God's worldwide spiritual mission. It has forever changed us.

And we get to see all this while allowing him to make our decisions. We're just along for the ride.

For those who submit to the authority of King Jesus, life could not be better, until he returns in triumph to consummate it all.

CHAPTER 5

EMBRACE THE MISSION OF KING JESUS

"Go and make disciples of all nations."
—MATTHEW 28:19

I met my son for dinner in January 2016. It was the last time I saw him before the worst day of my life.

He was away in college, and I had made the five-hour drive to visit him, take him out to dinner, and check on him. I knew he wasn't doing well. As we sat there, he had very little to say. His affect was flat. His face was blank. He had a perennial sadness in his eyes.

I've lost him. That's all I could think.

I've been a minister for decades. Both of my children grew up knowing the church inside and out. We participated in Christian ministries, attended Christian events, listened to Christian music, read Christian books, had Christian friends, and they attended (at times) Christian schools.

But Jonathan, my son, began to lose faith in God sometime during his teenage years. I still don't know if I can say what went wrong, but it probably had something to do his feeling that God didn't hear his prayers. He had severe depression for years. He suffered social anxiety. He lived in a dark place.

I remember vividly the day when he was fourteen and came to me and told me that he no longer believed. "I believe the Christian religion is still good, and I still respect you, Dad, but I don't think I believe anymore." I told him that I would pray for him. I told him that God would not stop pursuing him. I told him I love him. And I informed him that no matter what he believed, I expected him to live a Christian lifestyle as long as he was in my house. If he lived with me, he would still honor Christian values and go to church.

But every Sunday I would see him standing in church with his mouth closed; he wouldn't sing. His depression grew worse. He appeared to go somewhere deep inside, and I had little access to him. My heart grieved the spiritual loss of my son.

In early March, now some years later, he was away in college. I was scheduled to meet him in Chattanooga for a concert on Friday. It was Thursday, and I wasn't thinking much about it. And then I got the call that changed everything.

It is difficult for me to write about what happened to provoke that call. It is painful, sad, and deeply personal, first for my son, then for my family. Allow me to say only that Jonathan had hit rock bottom, and the nurse on the phone told me that I needed to come immediately. I called my wife, and we drove to my son's college town. By the time we got there, things had gone from bad to worse. We cried. We prayed. We begged God for our son.

After nearly a week there, we brought Jonathan home with us. He went upstairs to bed. All I could pray, over and over again, was the same prayer: "God, please save my son. Please."

I thought I had raised my son well. We never missed church. I had taught him to love and respect God. I had been generous and fair to him. How could he have lost Jesus and ended up so despondent?

KING JESUS MADE DISCIPLES, NOT MERE CHURCH MEMBERS

When someone you love as much as I love my son loses faith, you analyze everything. What had I done wrong? Why had I—a minister for decades—failed my own son? I began to wonder: Rather than raising Jonathan to love Jesus, had I raised him to be only a church member? And consequently, did he stop believing in Jesus because he stopped feeling connected to the church?

Had I missed the mark by neglecting to help my own son become a disciple of Jesus rather than a mere church member?

When Jesus came announcing the kingdom of God, the book of Matthew tells us, his first act was to call disciples.

Note the grammar of Matthew's gospel. In chapter 4, Jesus "began" to announce the arrival of the kingdom (v. 17), and the very next thing he did was to call Peter, Andrew, James, and John to become his disciples (vv. 18–22). The structure of this passage is important. Beginning to announce the kingdom of God involves the calling of disciples who are trained to make other disciples. The first thing Jesus did in inaugurating the kingdom was to make disciples who would make other disciples. So if we are to live in the kingdom of God, we must learn to become disciples who make disciples. That's how the kingdom spreads. That's what we do.

This makes sense. In the Lord's Prayer, Jesus says to the Father, "Your kingdom come, your will be done, on earth as it is in heaven" (Matt. 6:10). This is a summary statement of what constitutes God's kingdom: the kingdom of God comprises any place where the will of God is being done. Since disciples of Jesus are the only ones who fully seek to do God's will, making disciples is the primary means for advancing the kingdom of God.

It's worth pondering this point for a moment. Jesus could have advanced his kingdom any way he wanted. He is, after all, king of the universe. He could have commandeered the capacious theater in Caesarea (which still holds twenty-five thousand people), called in his friend Billy Graham, and hosted a crusade. He could have emblazoned a comet with the story of salvation and had it circle the world. He could have hopped across the continents on the wings of an angel, speaking to every tribe of people.

He didn't.

Instead he spent most of his time with twelve ordinary men, training them, equipping them, loving them, and teaching them to do God's will on earth as it is in heaven. Then Jesus commissioned them to go and do the same. Establishing the kingdom of God is the purpose of Jesus' incarnation. But making disciples was Jesus' chosen method for doing this. It was his mission.

Jesus came announcing the kingdom and then spent the rest of his life making disciples. In a similar way, if we are to follow Jesus, we too will become disciples who make disciples. It is in the final command of Jesus: "Go and make disciples of all nations." Making disciples is the mission of the church, and it should be the mission of every member of the church. Our becoming disciples who make disciples is how the kingdom of God spreads. We make disciples. It's what we do in the kingdom of God.

Or we fail.

The imperative to make disciples is found not only in Matthew's gospel. Some version of this Great Commission is found in all four gospels as well as in the book of Acts. At the close of Mark's gospel, Jesus says, "Go into all the world and preach the gospel to all creation. Whoever believes and is baptized will be saved, but whoever does not believe will be condemned" (Mark 16:15–16). At the end of Luke's gospel, Jesus says, "This is what is written: The Messiah will suffer and rise from the dead on the third day, and repentance for the forgiveness of sins will be preached in his name to all nations, beginning at Jerusalem. You are witnesses of these things" (Luke 24:46–48). In the last part of John's gospel, Jesus says, "As the Father has sent me, I am sending you" (John 20:21). And just prior to his ascension in the book of Acts, Jesus' final words are these: "You will receive power when the Holy Spirit comes on you; and you will be my witnesses in Jerusalem, and in all Judea and Samaria, and to the ends of the earth" (Acts 1:8).

The spiritual loss of my son was not an indictment of my ministry or my church. It did, however, strongly suggest to me that somewhere we had failed. My church operates more than a hundred ministries. We have strong Sunday services and spend lots of money to keep them strong. We support Christian schools; my son had attended one. We read Christian books to our children. Many mornings when they were growing up, we had devotionals before school. We went to Christian events and had Christian guests in our home all the time. But somehow all our programming and activities had missed my own son. It wasn't an indictment of me or my church, but it did tell me something that you need to know too.

You see, I had focused for years on making good church members. I had been interested in maintaining our programs, building the institution of my church, and watching our numbers grow. But in all the projects and busyness, I had failed to think seriously about how to make disciples. A church member is someone who comes to church. A good church member is someone who helps you build up the institution of church. But neither of these requires—believe it or not—being a real disciple. For though disciples of Jesus will certainly be part of a church, one doesn't have to be a serious disciple of Jesus to be a member of the church. For this reason, the focus of ministry should be to train individuals to trust and follow King Jesus, not merely to build up our institutions. We don't use people to build an institution; we use the institution to build up people. I think that to some degree I have had this backward for much of my life. A church is worthy of its existence only if it is building disciples of Jesus Christ. Making disciples is the mission of the church. And there is no other mission.

This is something of an oversimplification, but allow me to present a comparison between mere church members and real disciples of Jesus. I have adapted this chart from my own discipler, Bobby Harrington, who has used it in several teaching venues.

Mere Church Members	Disciples of Jesus
Go to church	Are the church
Talk about Jesus	Follow Jesus
Have doctrines about the Holy Spirit	Are led by the Holy Spirit
Pray for what they want	Pray for what God wants
Believe miracles might be possible	Experience miracles
Have done a study of demons	Have wrestled with demons
Are resistant to change	Are constantly growing

(cont.)

Mere Church Members	Disciples of Jesus
Know facts about God	Know God
Have strong preferences about church music	Sing
Listen to and critique sermons	Are living sermons
Live with secret sins and addictions	Confess their sins to be healed
Seek to raise successful children	Seek to raise Christlike children
Ask how they can be happy in their marriage	Ask how they can be Christ in their marriage
Make happiness their life mission	Make disciple making their life mission

It is important to remember that I was not accidentally focused on making church members. My system was perfectly designed to achieve exactly the result I was getting. If your church focuses on building up the institution of the church, thinking in terms of mere church members, that's what you'll get—an institution of mere members. But if your church focuses on making disciples, which is much harder but infinitely more rewarding, you'll get real, live followers of Jesus.

My son's experience helped me see clearly that I really had fallen into the trap of thinking that my job was to build my congregation rather than to spend my congregation for the sake of making disciples. And it did indict me personally. My mission in life had been to be the best church builder I could be. I wanted to be the best public speaker I could be. I wanted my church to love me. But I had never really taken seriously the mission of Jesus to make disciples of all nations. And I had not really challenged my church to take on this mission. And now I realize that. I still love and care for the institution of my congregation, but I no longer focus on saving it. I have learned that it is far better to spend my church in the mission of making disciples of all nations. And oddly, the more I seek to spend my church, the more Jesus saves it.

SO HOW DO WE MAKE DISCIPLES?

Henry Ford changed the world when he invented the automated assembly line. And what a gift his invention has been to humanity! Without it, you would never have been able to afford most of what you own. Even the printing of this book would have been cost prohibitive without the automated assembly line.

But unfortunately, the automated assembly line has become more than just a production model for industry in North America. It has also become a cultural posture. Our churches falsely believe that we can follow the assembly-line model and end up with personal disciples of Jesus. We falsely believe that we can make real disciples through strong programs, attractional weekend services, flashy events, fantastic music, and golden sermons. But it doesn't work that way. It didn't in Jesus' life. And it won't in yours either.

Mere church members can be mass-produced, but disciples cannot. To make disciples, we must return to the methods of Jesus. Jesus handcrafted disciples a small batch at a time. Disciples are handcrafted, or they are not made at all.

As far as we know, King Jesus never built an awesome Sunday service. He never started a ministry. He never had a budget, a church building, printed literature, a television program, or an awesome band. Instead of these, Jesus chose to build an intense relationship with a handful of men, leading them from spiritual infancy to full maturity. He didn't disciple remotely, on an assembly line, or through a program. And he didn't just throw out random seed, hoping it would flourish. He lovingly entered the lives of twelve ordinary men and led them to become like him. Jesus made disciples relationally.

This method proves to be slow; disciple making is a focused and labor-intensive process. But ask yourself how real heart change occurs in you. Doesn't it take time, discipline, and lots of determination? Doesn't it generally occur in the context of relationships?

Jesus spent enormous time with the disciples. Jesus spent time in their homes (Matt. 8:14). He met the disciples at their work (Matt. 8:23). He joined them for dinner (Matt. 9:10). He called them his true family (Matt. 12:49–50).

He sent them out to preach (Matt. 10:1–5). He challenged them to do ministry (Mark 6:37). He connected them to one another in loving relationships (John 13:34–35). Whenever he preached publicly, he took them aside and explained things to them privately (Mark 4:33–34). He shared life with them. And they became like him.

Jesus invested in the lives of twelve ordinary men; then, after he had poured into them for three years—even losing one to a painful betrayal—these men went forth and changed the world. They became so critical to the kingdom of God that their names—the names of twelve ordinary men—are inscribed on the foundations of the New Jerusalem (Rev. 21:14)!

Jesus did not make mere church members, as I had learned to do. He preached to crowds, yes. But he spent most of his time investing his life in the lives of twelve men to train them to become like him. Then he told them to go and do the same. When he commanded them to make disciples, they understood that he now wanted them to go and invest in the lives of a handful of other people as he had done for them. What else could he possibly have meant? He defined disciple making by his own life—investing in a handful of men to change them forever.

If we are going to follow Jesus, we also will invest in the lives of others to lead them to become like him. Why should we believe that the message of Jesus is perfect but not believe that his method is also perfect? Why should we believe in who he is but not adopt the mission he bears?

I recently visited a disciple-making movement that has brought hundreds of thousands of people to King Jesus. The movement is less than twenty years old, but already it has planted as many as twenty thousand churches and brought more than 1.5 million people to the kingdom of God, including more than 750,000 former Muslims. Through this movement, more Muslims have come to Christ in the last fourteen years than had come to Christ in the last fourteen centuries. Times ten!

I saw schools where children could get a solid Christian education for a dollar a month. I saw wells dug for fresh water in remote villages where there hadn't been fresh water since the garden of Eden. I interacted with people who had adopted or were fostering children who had no parents. Members of the movement were in the process of building a university. They had built clinics across their region and helped with agricultural projects. They had a Christian radio station that broadcast Christian messages, Christian music, and even a Christian comedian across the country.

But these kingdom works were only the result of the real engines of the movement. For the real power of this movement was found in the exact modeling of disciple making that King Jesus pioneered. The movement always starts with prayer, but then each and every member of the movement begins to pour into the lives of their friends, inviting them to Bible studies, teaching them about Jesus, baptizing them, then challenging them to go and do the same with their friends. Hundreds of thousands have become believers in fewer than twenty years because of it. Imagine this: every single one of these believers has the audacity to obey King Jesus and personally make disciples! They make disciples who make disciples. They don't make mere church members.

Now, when everyone is involved in making disciples, everything changes. In miraculous ways.

One Sunday morning, our little group of Westerners attended the largest church in the movement. There were hundreds of excited worshipers gathered. They started with Discovery Bible Study, a method of reading the Bible that invites immediate obedience to the Word of God and opens doors for disciple making. Then they began their music. I knew it would be big; our hosts had advised us to bring earplugs because the music would rock more than anything we had ever heard. They were right. The music was as big as a Super Bowl halftime performance.

As the people were singing, dancing, and praising God, I couldn't help but notice one man who was particularly animated. He was across the aisle from me and wearing a full black suit. He not only shouted out his songs of praise but danced without a care in the world. He was elated to worship his God. I saw him jumping, twisting, turning, shoving his hands upward, kneeling, lying flat on the floor, crying, and laughing.

I mentioned the young man to someone after the services, making some comment about how happy he looked. "Yeah," one of my hosts responded. "He used to be a member of Boko Haram, the Muslim terrorist organization over in Nigeria. The first time he came to one of our services, he came to figure out where best to detonate a suicide bomb among us. But someone met him and began to disciple him. Because of the power of the Bible, the prayers of the church, and a brother's commitment to disciple him, he has now given his life over to King Jesus. And he is currently making disciples of former Muslims and even planted churches among them. He's got a lot to sing about."

A few days later I saw him again. This time I instinctively went up to him and gave him a hug. A chill ran down my spine. "Imagine this," I whispered to myself. "I'm hugging a Boko Haram terrorist who first came to kill me. And now he is planting churches for King Jesus."

That's the power of making disciples as King Jesus did. An assembly line would not have changed this man. Nor would mere church membership. But having someone who loves you enough to enter your life and lead you to follow Jesus can change everything.

MAKING DISCIPLE MAKING YOUR MISSION

Any given year, there are as many as a million boys who play football in some sort of league—Little League, middle school, high school. Of this million, only about twenty-five thousand will go on to play college football, and of this number, less than five hundred will make it to the NFL in any given year. In the NFL, there will be only thirty-two starting quarterbacks. And of these thirty-two starting quarterbacks, only a handful will ever play in the Super Bowl. So what are the odds that two brothers would be starting quarterbacks with Super Bowl wins under their belts?

Almost zero.

Unless your father happens to have been Archie Manning, a former professional quarterback who discipled two of his sons to become world-class quarterbacks.

It's one of the most amazing feats in sports history. Archie Manning trained two of his sons so well that they both eventually won Super Bowls. Peyton and Eli Manning are a testimony to their father's skill, but they are also testimonies to the power of relational discipling.

You see, one man (Archie) loved two men (Eli and Peyton) enough to enter their lives relationally and bring out the Super Bowl player in them. He ate with them. He traveled with them. He met their friends, gave them opportunities to play, supplied their needs, and coached them. And how many aspiring quarterbacks have now been discipled by Eli and Peyton?

The world desperately needs people who love others enough to enter their lives and to lead them to become world-class followers of King Jesus. And you are called to have this kind of love. You should make disciple making a personal priority—a mission in your life. It's surprising how many of us have never even considered this.

I once surveyed 150 Christian adults, asking them what they understand the mission of the church to be. I then asked them what they understand the mission of their lives to be.

Only a couple of them responded that the mission of the church is to make disciples. That alone made me sad. But get this: not a single respondent included disciple making in the mission of their personal lives. Not a single one.

It's sad how many don't realize that the mission of the church is to make disciples of all nations. But it's bizarre that even those who do can fail to personalize that mission. Let me assure you that if you have a church full of people whose mission in life is everything but making disciples, you are not going to get a church that makes disciples.

One church that has successfully bucked this trend is Real Life Ministries in Post Falls, Idaho. Post Falls feels like a long way from anywhere because it is a long way from most places. One of its founding pastors, Jim Putman, started out his adult life as a wrestling coach. After leaving Christ for some part of his life, he returned, but he wanted to come back to a "winning team," as he explained it. So he asked the hard question of what a score looks like in his life, as well as in the kingdom of God. He concluded that a score occurs every time a person becomes like Jesus. He concluded that this is the only score that matters in his life. So he committed his life to relational discipleship, and he built a church on this mission.[13]

Starting with a handful of people whom he personally discipled, Putman trained people to go make other disciples. Several decades later, in a city that has fewer than thirty thousand inhabitants, Real Life ministries has eight thousand members. Everyone who attends knows that they are expected to make disciples. And the church has sent out many disciple makers to other places. Lots of them have planted other disciple-making churches. It's now just in their culture.

Anywhere you see the kingdom of God flourishing today, you can be sure that people are making disciple making a priority. We are living in the most explosive period of growth in the entire history of Christianity; we just don't see it in the West. But across Africa, in the Middle East and India, and across China and Southeast Asia, people are coming to Jesus by the millions. It's ironic, because Christians in these places typically have very little access to the church luxuries we enjoy in the West: great Sunday services, large budgets, professional speakers, public ministries, Christian bookstores, radio stations, and schools. What they do have, however, is enough love to adopt Jesus' mission for the lost world: they make disciples, one by one.

If you've ever wondered how the early church went from a handful of people to become a world religion, the answer is through relational disciple making. Years ago, in his *Book of Martyrs*, John Foxe neatly summarized how this disciple-making process won the day. Speaking of the Roman world, Foxe wrote, "In that age every Christian was a missionary. The soldier tried to win recruits for the heavenly host; the prisoner sought to bring his jailer to Christ; the slave girl whispered the gospel in the ears of her mistress; the young wife begged her husband to be baptized that their souls might not be parted after death; every one who had experienced the joys of believing tried to bring others to the faith."[14]

So not only should the mission of the church be that of making disciples, but the mission of your life should include that of making disciples. So how do you proceed?

Many of us believe that disciple making is reserved only for the professionals, but this is wrong. The opposite is true. Disciple making by every ordinary Christian should be the norm. Think of Peyton Manning again. He didn't start playing football the day he made it to his first Super Bowl. He started when he was three years old, before he could even hold a football in one hand. My Jonathan learned to read when he was four years old, because his six-year-old sister was in school learning to read, and she had the time and interest in sharing with her brother. We should start making disciples as soon as we accept the authority of King Jesus. How many degrees must a person have to teach a four-year-old how to read? Strictly speaking, none. A four-year-old can learn to read if he has a six-year-old who loves him enough to disciple him. I know you are at least six years old.

In the same way, you start making disciples by, well, making disciples. Sure, you need good training to become your best at it. But anyone who trusts and follows King Jesus should begin immediately loving others enough to enter into their lives and help them trust and follow Jesus as well.

How do we do this? Let me again quote from my own discipler, Bobby Harrington, who is also the founder and executive director of Discipleship.org. Bobby has identified seven key rhythms essential for effectively making disciples.[15] Each of them is taken directly from the model Jesus has left us.

First, we fast and pray that God will lead us to the people we should disciple. These might be people who don't know King Jesus. Or they could be people who have been church members for years. They may be our family members, neighbors, coworkers, or even ministers. God will lead you where he wants you to go, if you ask. Pray, and then open your eyes.

Second, we invite those to whom God has led us into a relationship. Our motivation is nothing other than love. We should love others enough to offer ourselves to them. To do this, consider inviting anywhere from two to eleven same-gendered people into a relationship, making a covenant with them, and then pouring yourself into their lives for the purpose of helping them become like Christ. Gather people who are willing to invest in intentional relationships. Consider how Jesus spent his time with his twelve disciples, and imitate him.

Even if you don't have all the answers, you can gather a group and allow the power of the Word of God to shape every person in the group.

Next, we establish a rhythm that will lead them to become like King Jesus. There are four elements to this rhythm, and they work well if you do each once or twice per month. Harrington numbers these elements three through six, after prayer and inviting along.

Third, we teach them the will of God through Bible study. There is immense power in the Word of God, and opening up the Word will transform people's lives in profound ways. At my congregation, we use Discovery Bible Study (DBS), a method shared with us by Final Command Ministries.[16] DBS offers anyone the opportunity to be molded by the Scriptures, because it consists of nothing but a series of questions about the Bible that leads us to listen to the Word, obey it, and share it with others. There are many resources available for listening to the Word of God. DBS is just one of them.[17]

Fourth, we share meals with each other. Just as Jesus did much of his discipling around a table, so we can also lovingly shape others' lives when we break bread with them in fellowship.

Fifth, we share ministry with each other. Almost everywhere that Jesus went and in almost every ministry he performed, the disciples were there, watching and learning. So when Jesus ascended into heaven, the disciples were fully prepared to take over his ministry.

Sixth, we rest together. We shouldn't underestimate the power of just recreating, playing, and resting with those whom we love. If you've raised children, you know that sometimes your best moments happen when you are relaxing with them.

These four monthly rhythms will create the relational garden in which discipleship can flourish.

Seventh, we commission our disciples to go make disciples of others. Since Jesus was a disciple maker who trained others to go make disciples, we can follow him fully only if we are disciple makers who train others to go make disciples. Effective disciple making occurs only when the disciples you lead become disciple makers themselves. Become a spiritual grandparent.

While there are lots of fantastic resources available for becoming a world-class disciple maker, remember that once you choose to follow King Jesus, you should begin learning the sport immediately. Jesus made disciples. So should you.

When Hurricane Harvey struck the Houston area of Texas, it inflicted the most damage ever done by a cyclone—$125 billion worth of destruction. Flooding was everywhere, and seventeen thousand people had to be rescued. More than a hundred people lost their lives.

One emotional rescue was captured on someone's cell phone. You can still watch it on YouTube, and you should, because it is amazing.[18]

An older gentleman had driven his truck into a rushing river, thinking it was just a puddle. Soon his truck was filling with water and appeared ready to be swept away. His life was in danger, and there was no rescue team in sight.

Then, out of the blue, a bystander shouted out for others to hold his hand. The video, which went viral, shows an entire group of random, ordinary people—Hispanic, African American, and Caucasian—forming a human chain reaching out to the truck. These were not members of a search-and-rescue team. They were not SWAT members or Navy Seals. They were just ordinary people who cared about a man at risk. Lining up and linking hands, a dozen people waded out into the torrent and pulled the gentleman out of the truck. He is seen being cradled by a rescuer at the end of the human chain, who gently brought him to safety in his arms that day. Even writing this sentence makes me choke up.

Imagine what the world would look like if every Christian viewed the mission of Jesus with the same passion. Imagine if—instead of living our lives for ourselves, locking our doors after supper every night, endlessly seeking recreation, entertainment, and luxury, treating church as something we do rather than someone we are—we decided to live up to our personal mission of making disciples of all nations. Imagine if our churches became living chains of people reaching out to a lost and drowning world and bringing people into the safety of the arms of King Jesus. Imagine if every one of us could say, with clarity and confidence, "The mission of my life is to make disciples of all nations."

The good news is that you can.

TO SING AGAIN

My son stayed in his room for more than a week, coming out for only short periods of time. His mother and I prayed. And worried. And prayed.

Since he had to drop out of college, I decided to pay my son a small salary from my own pocket to work with the producer of my church's television program. Jonathan loves cameras, and he didn't have anything else to do. But unbeknownst to my son, our producer is a world-class disciple maker who believes that making films is only a tool for making disciples. He immediately began to disciple my son.

Then another of our staff members gave me a call.

In a providential twist of fate, we had recently hired a grand master in tae kwon do as a minister for my church. He asked my permission to take my son out to lunch. Then he asked my son if he wanted to earn a black belt in tae kwon do. "If you will work with me every day," he promised, "I will give you a black belt in record time. Six months. If you meet with me every day and work hard."

Both men discipled my son, meeting with him pretty much every day. They used their arts to enter my son's life—camera work and tae kwon do were "access ministries." Eventually the producer left his job with the church to pursue a film-making career, but not before getting into the soul of my son.

During the first few months, I didn't notice much difference in my son, but he did seem to be getting out of his depression. Somewhere in the middle of his martial arts training, my son invited me to attend a demonstration in which he broke a number of boards. At the end of the session, unexpectedly and without explanation, the grand master had my son lay hands on me and pray over me. I broke into tears. When we got home, I thanked my son for the prayer. "I'm glad you liked it. I still don't know what I believe, but Sensei made me do it. He makes me pray with him every day."

Soon, however, I noticed deep changes in my son's life. Though he had gone to Christian schools, had been in Christian circles, had grown up with daily family devotionals, and had listened to fine Christian preaching (I'm joking), he still lost his faith in our programmatic, event-centered, listen-to-me model of doing church. The assembly line of my church had not been adequate. But when two men loved my son enough to pour their lives into his, he began to find Jesus again.

One of the best days of my life occurred when my son received his black belt. A crowd of us were there to witness it. He did several performances, broke a number of boards, did a hundred push-ups in less than two minutes, held his leg above his head for what seemed like forever, and generally proved that he was worthy. My son earned the black belt in tae kwon do in a shorter amount of time than virtually anyone else in the history of tae kwon do. The sensei took his own black belt off and gave it to my son.

Then my son addressed the crowd, telling us what he'd experienced for the last six months. He spoke of how much his life had changed and how grateful he was for the two disciplers. Then he looked me straight in the eye and said, "Dad, you remember the conversation we had where I told you I didn't think I believed?" I nodded. "Well, I'm back. And I believe Jesus Christ is my Lord and Savior."

There is no way to describe what I felt.

But that's not all. My son soon began to do so much ministry that we moved him out of television production and onto the ministry staff. He started a school of disciple making, training sixty more people how to make disciples. He began working for a church plant, sponsored by our church, on the campus of our local university. He even married the women's campus minister there, a wonderful woman who is also a serious disciple of King Jesus. He has become an excellent Bible scholar. He personally leads five discipleship groups. He has baptized a lot of people, including some of his best friends from both high school and college days. And as I write this, my twenty-four-year-old son is making final plans to lead a church plant team to the great American Northwest for King Jesus.

And one day not that long ago, I was standing in church next to him. I looked over at him in teary-eyed gratitude.

He was singing.

CHAPTER 6

IMMERSE YOURSELF IN THE LIFE OF KING JESUS

"Baptizing them in the name of the Father
and of the Son and of the Holy Spirit."

—MATTHEW 28:19

Here's a tale of two buggies.

The Tyson and Jones Buggy Company began making horse-drawn buggies out of Carthage, North Carolina, in 1850. Because of their hardworking employees and their high-quality design, they soon became the largest buggy company in the South, manufacturing as many as three thousand carriages per year. Theirs were the Cadillac buggies of the day.

Around the same time, the Durant-Dort Carriage Company was producing similar buggies out of Flint, Michigan. Founded in 1886, Durant-Dort soon grew even larger than Tyson and Jones, becoming the largest carriage company in America and selling nearly ten times more buggies than Tyson and Jones.

Soon, as you have already guessed, both companies faced an insurmountable challenge—the automobile. And here's where the story gets interesting.

You see, Tyson and Jones was in the *buggy* business. Their entire mindset was built around producing the finest buggy in the world. They studied buggies, pioneered new styles of buggies, and focused all of their attention on buggies. Consequently, when the automobile became popular, Tyson and Jones went bankrupt. They reportedly sold their last buggy to an eighty-year-old man who swore he would never drive an automobile. The year was 1925.

Meanwhile the Durant-Dort Carriage Company was in the *transportation* business. Sure, they knew a lot about buggies, but they didn't just study buggies.

They studied transportation. They knew about people. They learned about travel needs, transportation trends, and market selection.

So even though Durant-Dort ceased making buggies around the same time as did Tyson and Jones, they didn't go out of business. Instead they morphed into an automobile company. Durant-Dort became a little corporation that today we like to call General Motors.

What was the difference between the two companies? Tyson and Jones considered itself a buggy company. Durant-Dort considered itself a transportation company. Knowing who they were made all the difference in the world. Today Tyson and Jones is just a historical marker in Carthage. General Motors employs nearly two hundred thousand people.

There's an immense amount of power that comes with knowing exactly who you are. There is power in clarity.

I once attended a John Maxwell seminar and listened to this Christian consultant discussed the ethical failings of several executives of a major U.S. corporation. Their manipulations of finances had led to the ruin of many investors and had landed several of the corporation's VIPs in prison. Then Maxwell was asked how ordinary people could make such extraordinarily bad decisions. "Because," Maxwell commented, "they never really decided who they are. Not knowing who they are left them unsure about what to do. So when the collective temptation came for them to cheat the numbers, they did the wrong thing."

When you fail to establish, once and for all, who you are, you set yourself up for constant failure. You equivocate at the moments when you should stand tall. You change your mind and splinter into a thousand directions. You stress yourself out, lose endless nights of sleep, and never achieve what your king designed you to achieve.

But the opposite is also true. When you establish, once and for all, who you are, you will also know what to do.

I once heard a story told by business guru Ken Blanchard, author of the once-famous book *One Minute Manager*. Blanchard was flying out of Miami to a speaking engagement somewhere in the Midwest. When he got to the airport counter, however, he realized he had forgotten his photo ID. He was already running late, and he knew that if he missed the flight, he would miss his speaking engagement. He pleaded with the desk manager to let him fly anyway, but security wouldn't allow it. Suddenly, getting a flash of brilliance, he ran down to the airport bookstore and bought a copy of a book he had coauthored with former Miami Dolphins head coach Don Shula, *Everyone's a Coach*. On the back cover of the book was a picture of Blanchard, standing next to Shula.

In Miami, as it happens, Don Shula is the size of Elvis. Or bigger. When the airline staff saw the picture, they began to shout, "We have a friend of Don Shula here!" Thrilled to know someone who knew Shula, they not only let Blanchard board the plane but upgraded him to first class!

Having a clear identity matters.

This is what baptism is all about. Baptism is the outward sign of our inward faith—our announcement to the whole world that we have drawn a line in the sand for King Jesus. It is our once-and-for-all declaration that we forevermore are citizens of his kingdom. And we are not going to back down.

Now, let's talk about baptism.

BAPTISM AS A ONCE-AND-FOR-ALL PLEDGE

Jesus' final command in Matthew's gospel is premised on the authority God has given him: "All authority in heaven and on earth has been given to me" (Matt. 28:18). In response to this authority, we are to become disciple makers: "Therefore go and make disciples of all nations" (v. 19).

Jesus goes on to explain that making disciples of all nations includes "baptizing them in the name of the Father and of the Son and of the Holy Spirit" (v. 19).

In some ways, it is strange that among Jesus' last and most important words is the command for us to baptize people. The English word baptism is only a loanword from Greek; it is just a transliteration of the Greek word *baptisma*. Were the term translated, it would mean something like "wash." To appreciate how odd the command is among

Jesus' most important words, here is what Matthew 28:19 looks like with the word *baptisma* translated rather than merely transliterated: "Go and make disciples of all nations, washing them in the name of the Father, Son, and Holy Spirit." Doesn't it sound a little odd to introduce the concept of washing into Jesus' last words?

To get an even better feel for its strangeness, imagine if Jesus had said, as his last words on earth, "Go make disciples, brushing their teeth."

What's going on in this text?

The short answer is that to become a disciple, we require a public washing in which we declare to the world that our old self is forever gone. Baptism is the act of announcing to everyone that we have drawn a line in the sand, have taken our stand with King Jesus, and will never back down. It is a public statement of who we are, from now on and forevermore. This is why baptism is so important. This is why Matthew 28 makes baptism the third imperative of obedience-based discipleship. It marks the decisive moment of our commitment to King Jesus, as other biblical texts also indicate.

In John 3:5, Jesus says that no one can enter the kingdom of God without first being born of water and the Spirit. Jesus' reference to the Spirit makes it clear that possessing the Holy Spirit is necessary for anyone who lives in his kingdom. But his reference to being "born of water" demonstrates that baptism is a sort of birth. It is an entrance point into the kingdom of God. Everyone is born as citizens into some kingdom. If we are to become citizens of God's kingdom, we must be born into it. Water baptism gives us that new birth.

Romans 6:3–4 teaches us that baptism is a symbol of dying, being buried, and then being raised with Christ into a new life. Paul is addressing sin and salvation in Romans 1–8, and he wants to illustrate why we must abandon any effort to earn our way into the kingdom and instead depend solely on faith in Jesus. One of his illustrations of this truth is that of baptism. We die to the old self when we are baptized. We are buried in the water of baptism. Then we are raised up from the water so that we can begin living a new kind of life. Water baptism is fundamentally dying to ourselves and living for King Jesus. It is a symbol of salvation by faith alone.

In 1 Peter 3:20–21, the apostle Peter mentions that Noah was saved by water, presumably meaning that the world was cleansed of its sinfulness by the flood, leaving Noah in a purified world. Then Peter explains that "this water symbolizes baptism that now saves you also—not the removal of dirt from the body but the pledge of a clear conscience toward God. It saves you by the resurrection of Jesus Christ" (v. 21). Baptism, Peter explains, is intended not to remove dirt from our body but to testify that our consciences have been cleaned. Baptism is, for the follower of Jesus, a symbol of the spiritual cleansing Jesus performs when we trust and follow him. It is a way of participation in the resurrection of Jesus himself.

In Acts 2:38–39, Peter answers the question that new believers asked him: "What must we do?" His answer echoes Jesus' final command in Matthew 28:19: "Repent and be baptized, every one of you, in the name of Jesus Christ for the forgiveness of your sins. And you will receive the gift of the Holy Spirit" (Acts 2:38). Here Peter connects baptism to the remission of sins and the gift of the Holy Spirit. Having our sins forgiven is necessary for us to enter a right relationship with God. And receiving the gift of the Holy Spirit is nothing short of receiving God himself into our hearts through the Spirit. Note that both of these gifts from God are linked to the washing that baptism symbolizes.

In each of these texts, baptism functions as a public symbol that declares our new allegiance to King Jesus. It is a line in the sand drawn for all to see.

Does this mean that water saves us? Absolutely not. The water is not what matters. It is the relationship with Jesus that matters, but entrance into that relationship is symbolized in our water baptism. Does this mean that a work—a deed of our own doing—saves us? No, for we are never saved by works. Remember that baptism is not something that I do. It is something that is done to me. I didn't baptize myself, and I didn't earn something in baptism. In the act of baptism, I yielded myself into someone else's hands. My minister baptized me when I was eight years old; all I did was lie down. And God in his amazing grace washed away my sins in baptism; I didn't earn a single degree of forgiveness. Baptism is not a work, and it does not earn me anything.

Baptism is simply a declaration that I have a new king in my life, that the old me has forever died and was even buried. From this point forward, I have risen to walk a new life. Baptism is my declaration of who I am, or better yet, whose I am. I take my stand from now on with King Jesus. No reserves. No retreats. No regrets.

Compare baptism with a wedding ceremony, as Bobby Harrington, Tony Twist, and I did in a book on baptism some time back.[19] A person is typically in love with their soon-to-be spouse long before the wedding. The wedding doesn't create the love. And one should be committed to another before the wedding too. The wedding doesn't create the commitment. But the wedding does consummate the love and declare it publicly. In the wedding ceremony, we declare and seal our love and our commitment to each other. And we state to the whole world that there is no turning back. We are, from that point forward, joined to one another. As millions of people have said in wedding services, "To have and to hold, from this day forward, till death do us part."

So it is with baptism. In his final command, King Jesus is teaching us that we should expect people to make a once-and-for-all decision to follow him, a decision that precludes any other kings and any further negotiation. In baptism we not only make this decision but declare it to the whole world.

It is not the water that is important. Your mother taught you to brush your teeth not because having brushes and paste are important. She taught you to brush your teeth because having teeth is important. We are baptized in the name of the Father, the Son, and the Holy Spirit not because water is important. We are baptized in the name of the triune God because making a once-and-for-all public commitment is important. And baptism is the means by which we declare and confirm that commitment. It is the point at which we die to our old selves, are buried, and then are raised to walk in newness of life. It is the line in the sand that declares everything has changed for us.

LIVING A BAPTIZED LIFE

Everybody dips their chips in salsa to their own beat. I scoop. My daughter dips. My wife dunks the same chip in the salsa over and over, soaking it before eating it.

If the New Testament had used the Greek verb *baptō* to describe baptizing, it would be a bit more like my daughter's dipping, for *baptō* means something like a one-time dip. But the New Testament doesn't use *baptō*. It prefers the verb *baptizō* (the verb from which *baptisma* comes). And whereas *baptō* means to dip, *baptizō* means to soak, slosh around, and even to marinate. Baptism in the Bible is akin to my wife's repeated marinating of her chip in salsa.

Why does this matter? Because, as I have already pointed out, the transactional view of Jesus falsely believes that salvation is a singular act that requires no further obedience to King Jesus. But biblical baptism is not just a dip in the water; it is a continual immersion in the life of Jesus. We are not called to have a baptismal transaction, as in a one-off dip in advance of an otherwise self-centered life. We are called to live baptized lives. Sure, it starts with a dip in water. But the washing is supposed to last; we are supposed to live in baptism. This is why Matthew 28:19 says we are baptized into the name of the Father, the Son, and the Holy Spirit. "Into" doesn't mean only "by the authority of." It means "in order to share a relationship with." We are to be sloshed around in Jesus. We are to be continually washed. We should be, if you can stand the metaphor, marinated in him. We are baptized not only by his authority but into a new relationship with him. Baptism is the visible symbol of a brand-new way of life. It is a washed life, a life in which you have died to yourself, have taken up a cross, and are now committed to following King Jesus.

The metaphor of marriage helps here again. If you ever married, odds are you exchanged wedding rings with your spouse. The wedding ring symbolizes several things, but most important, it declares to everybody else that you are committed and are no longer available. You may have put the ring on only once, during the wedding. But you now wear the ring every day, to declare that you are in a lifelong relationship. Baptism is the wedding ring of following Jesus. You may be dipped only once, but it is intended to signify that you are permanently married to King Jesus. You are no longer available for any other god, including the god of self.

But we must be honest here. Many of us are still unsure about our commitment to King Jesus. Allow me to demonstrate by using variations on the theme of baptism.

Sprinkled Disciples

Some of us are merely sprinkled with King Jesus. We may have started with a strong feeling—a response to a passionate altar call or a sense that we needed a new direction. Often it was in a moment of conviction or guilt. We acted by saying the sinner's prayer, by being baptized, or by coming forward to the altar at church. But sprinkled disciples have never really internalized the self-denial and cross-bearing call of Jesus, so they still live their lives for themselves. Self-denial makes no sense to them. And carrying a cross? That is the exact opposite of what sprinkled disciples seek for their lives.

They were sprinkled with Jesus, but they were never really immersed in him. They are mere cultural Christians.

So sprinkled disciples compromise, negotiate, and use King Jesus. He is there to help them get what they want. If you want to know whether you are a mere sprinkled disciple, ask yourself if you can honestly pray the Jesus prayer: "Lord, please don't do what I want; instead, from this point on I accept what you want." How you answer that question will tell what kind of baptism you've had.

Jim Putman and Bobby Harrington have summarized the pervasiveness of mere cultural Christianity. "The divorce rates between Christians and non-Christians is about the same, the percentage of men who read pornography is roughly the same, Christians are considered to be more than 2 times as likely to have racist attitudes than non-Christians. Domestic violence, drug abuse, and alcohol abuse are just as prevalent among Christians as non-Christians. One in four people living together outside of marriage call themselves evangelicals. Only 6% of evangelicals regularly tithe and only about half the people who say they regularly attend church, actually do. 60%–80% of people leave church in their twenties."[20]

Putman and Harrington's numbers indicate that cultural Christians live lives virtually indistinguishable from those of nonbelievers. Here's an example.

Becky is a sprinkled disciple. She goes to church, but not too much. Baptized as a teenager, she got her "fire insurance." Now she can live her life for herself, feeling secure that she will also have a great life after she dies. She is obsessed with how she looks. She loves her expensive luxuries. She wants a pampered life.

She married to find happiness, and if her husband, Ted, ever stops making her happy, she'll just move on to another marriage. For Becky, it's all about her. Jesus is just here to help her have a good life.

Here's the sad thing about Becky. By living for herself, she is missing out on the fantastic adventure that King Jesus has offered her. Real miracles cluster around real discipleship. Those who have a watered-down faith generally do not experience the great power, beauty, and thrill of a life walked with King Jesus. Worse, those who have a watered-down faith are still in bondage. And so, although she appears to have it all together, Becky is in bondage, and when she puts her head on her pillow at night, she knows it. She is in bondage to anger, unforgiveness, low self-esteem, feelings of failure, endless discouragement, and loneliness. All of these are the very things from which King Jesus wants to set her free! He offers her the fruit of the Spirit: love, joy, peace, goodness, and the like. But to have this fruit, she must surrender her will to the will of the Father. And that is something she is unwilling to do.

Voluntary slavery is still, in the end, slavery. Sprinkled disciples volunteer to remain captive to the world, their lusts and passions, and their own designs. They are willing slaves. So they remain in bondage. All while King Jesus is inviting them to be set free.

Dipped Disciples

Some Christians have studied the life of self-denial and cross-bearing, but they have never fully decided to live it. Dipped in Jesus, they have made basic commitments to a Christian life. They go to church. They join a small group. They read their Bible. They even listen to Christian music. But they are like the seed thrown among thorns and thistles in Jesus' parable of the sower. They sprout faith, but when the cares, riches, or pleasures of life arise, their faith is choked out (Luke 8:14). I don't mean that they stop going to church or praying. They often continue the rhythms of faith way beyond the point where any realness has ceased to exist. Life goes on, even after the thrill of living is gone.

James is one of these dipped disciples. He was raised in church and has served as a small group leader, a deacon, and even occasionally a Bible class leader.

But somewhere along the way, he got his feelings hurt when his church didn't "honor his leadership," as he describes it. Actually, there were many things that he didn't like at church. Rather than trying to work these out as a follower of King Jesus, he ultimately just resigned all his positions and stubbornly crossed his spiritual arms. Now he largely lives for himself. His work takes up most of his mental energy. He is building onto his house. He treats his family well enough, but they never see him pray, serve, or sacrifice. If he were the only thing they knew about King Jesus, they would conclude that Jesus is not very important.

Dipped disciples are typically those who started strong. They had passion. They had a vision. But the difficulties of living faithfully eventually led them to tap out. Allow me to use a military analogy.

Training for the U.S. Navy Seals is as grueling as you would expect. The recruits are subject to intensive physical challenges, extreme danger, mental and emotional stress, and the taunts of their trainers. They receive very little sleep. They are stretched to their limits.

Throughout the months of testing, a large bell hangs from a porch at the training grounds. Anytime a recruit wants, he or she can tap out, ring the bell, and enjoy a donut and coffee. They can call it quits. The trainers invite the recruits to ring the bell. They point to it and talk about it. They taunt and tease the recruits. And many recruits do tap out and ring the bell. The training is just too hard for them.

In the same way, living for King Jesus can be difficult, painful, and exhausting, especially in a selfish, pagan world. And all the while we are trying to serve King Jesus, the evil one has hung a bell in front of us, and he, like the Navy Seals trainers, invites us to tap out. He invites us to give up on the hard work of living for Jesus. He taunts us and teases us. And though he is fine if we continue to go to church, identify as Christian, and hold generic Christian values, he endlessly tells us that it is too hard to give our lives fully to King Jesus. And so while many continue to wear the uniform of discipleship, they have long since rung they bell. They are merely dipped disciples.

But the best of the kingdom of God is reserved for those who are fully immersed in King Jesus.

Immersed Disciples

The last words of King Jesus in Matthew's gospel include the command that we baptize in the name of the Father, Son, and Holy Spirit. Jesus wants us not only to be dipped in the kingdom but also to marinate in it, to immerse ourselves in King Jesus. This is what the parables of the hidden treasure and the pearl of great price demonstrate. In the first of these, Jesus describes a man who discovers a hidden treasure buried in a field. He goes home and sells everything he has and buys the field (Matt. 13:44). In the second parable, Jesus compares the kingdom of God to a jeweler who finds the perfect pearl. Recognizing the pearl's worth, the jeweler sells every stone he has to purchase this one pearl (Matt. 13:45–46). In both parables, Jesus is teaching us that once we discover who he is, we are to sell everything and take up only him and his kingdom. We are to live baptized lives.

Dalton and Jenna are examples of fully immersed disciples. They are members of my congregation.

A young married couple, they were thrilled several years ago when they found out Jenna was pregnant with their second child. About fourteen weeks into her pregnancy, Jenna went to the doctor for a routine checkup. While there, she decided to add a lab-drawn blood sample to learn her baby's gender. She was hoping to surprise her husband by announcing the baby's gender to him on his birthday. Returning home from the doctor, she waited for the call.

The call came, but it was not the good news she was expecting. The nurse said, "You need to come in. There is a problem." Jenna hurried to the doctor's office, where she was told that she was pregnant with a little girl, but her daughter had trisomy 13, a rare genetic disorder that produces severe abnormalities and disabilities. "Your little girl is incompatible with life," the doctor told her.

Jenna and Dalton were devastated. Not sure what to do next, they asked for expert advice. Several advised them to terminate the pregnancy. Even though their baby was not in pain, she would probably never make it to birth. And if she did, she would die shortly thereafter.

Because Jenna and Dalton are fully immersed in King Jesus, they took seriously his commands and teachings in Scripture about the value of every human life. Every human life is made in the image of God. For them, and for me, that includes human lives at every stage of development, which in turn meant that abortion was never an option for them. "There is no way," Jenna told me, "that we were going to take the life of our little girl." Jenna was determined to carry her daughter to full term. She and Dalton named their girl Evelynn.

Every day they endured the grief, but they took joy in feeling Evelynn move around. They often spoke to her and reassured her that they loved her and would never leave her. They wept. And prayed. And grieved. But they also reassured. And touched. And loved.

Four weeks before she was to be born, little Evelynn passed away. Her broken-hearted parents got only a brief chance to hold their daughter before handing her over to the hospital staff for burial. But they knew that they would see her again, at the return of King Jesus. At the resurrection, when, as Jesus says, all things will be made new (Rev. 21:5).

This is what it looks like when you know who you are. When we make a commitment to trust and follow Jesus, we also decide, once and for all, who we are. This is a very important truth, for when we know who we are, we will also know what we should do. Many of us have only been tourists in the kingdom of God. We have lived within its boundaries, but we never really made a full commitment to it. So, unsure of whether we're fully in, we are also unsure of what we will do. People who don't have a clear image of who they are never really know what to do.

But those who are living fully immersed lives can face tragedy, hardship, self-sacrifice, and opposition with confidence. They know what to do, because they know who they are.

YOUR LINE-IN-THE-SAND MOMENT

In the second century before Christ, Antiochus, the hubristic ruler of the Seleucid Empire, decided to capture Egypt with its vast fields of grain. He had only one problem: Rome. The Romans knew that if Antiochus controlled the breadbasket of the world, Rome itself would be threatened. Antiochus marched his army south and encircled the leading city of Egypt, Alexandria.

It was too late for Rome to send an army to confront Antiochus, so the Romans hurriedly sent a legate (a high-ranking political appointee), Gaius Popilius Laenas, to stop Antiochus. Arriving in Alexandria only a few days before Antiochus's armies began to lay siege, Laenas had no weapons, no strong allies, and, worst of all, no army. But he did have the power of Rome behind him. And he carried a threat from Rome: leave Egypt or face the might of the Roman legions.

Confronting Antiochus outside of Alexandria, Laenas told him to leave Egypt. Antiochus was furious. How could Rome be so brash? Who did Leanas think he was, ordering around Antiochus's conquering army? What could Rome do?

Antiochus informed the Roman legate that he would have to think about Rome's ultimatum. He would retire to his camp and consult his officials. Then, to everyone's surprise, the Roman legate did something that would live forever in the annals of history. Taking a stick, Laenas drew a circle in the sand around the feet of Antiochus. Looking Antiochus in the eye, Leanas said, "You'll give your answer before you step out of this circle."

And there you have it—the origin of the term "line in the sand." A moment of decision that changes everything.

Antiochus backed down, left Egypt, and later became infamous for provoking and losing a war with the Maccabees in Israel. His life ended in obscurity. Rome went on to conquer the West.

History is filled with such line-in-the-sand moments. One need only think of Martin Luther's refusal to back down to the Roman Catholic Church, or Rosa Parks's refusal to move to the back of a bus. In each case, someone drew a line in the sand, refused to cross it, and changed the course of history.

Your baptism is your line-in-the-sand moment. It is your opportunity to say, once and for all, that you take your stand in King Jesus and you will not back down, so help you God. Only that kind of commitment changes the earth. Only that kind of commitment opens the eyes of the blind.

That's what Ibrahim told me.

Ibrahim grew up in a village in the countryside of Liberia. His entire village was Muslim, and his father expected him to take the faith seriously too. So he did. By the time he was in his twenties, Ibrahim knew the Koran intimately and was teaching it to others. He quickly became the local Muslim sheik (an Islamic spiritual leader), with authority over the whole village.

But something happened to Ibrahim. He developed an eye disease, and suddenly he was unable to read the Koran. The villagers whispered that he must have done something to offend Allah. As his eyesight grew quickly worse, he was asked to resign as the sheik of the village. He fell into a deep depression. Everything that had mattered to him was going up in smoke, including his eyesight.

At the same time and by sheer coincidence, Ibrahim was leasing a room in his house to a young man who was in the village for business. The young man was a disciple of King Jesus. Seeing Ibrahim's despair, he invited him to come to his Bible study and have the Christians pray over him. Ibrahim's eyesight didn't improve, but for the first time Ibrahim felt true acceptance and joy. The Christians even paid for him to have surgery to recover his sight, although the surgery was unsuccessful. Ibrahim remained blind, but now he had a loving family.

After intensive prayer and listening to the Christian Scriptures, Ibrahim could no longer keep himself from Jesus. Without ever having seen a Bible, Ibrahim obeyed the Bible and gave his life to Jesus. He was baptized in a river, making a public declaration to live a life immersed in King Jesus, whatever the cost.

And the cost was high. Ibrahim's family disowned him, and threats were made against his life; a fatwa (death threat) was issued against him. But Ibrahim had drawn a line in the sand. He was going to stand with King Jesus. There was no going back. In Jesus, he said, he found real love, real joy, and real light. He had declared his commitment to Jesus, once and for all. He moved south to join a Christian church.

But what to do with his life? All Ibrahim had ever done was teach the Koran. He could no longer read, so he didn't feel that he could become a Bible scholar. The one thing he could do, however, was pray. So he began to fast and pray. At first he didn't even know what to say. In his first several prayers, he got the name Jesus wrong. But eventually his prayers became so powerful that people started coming to him and asking him to pray over them. Many were healed. Lives were transformed. Amazing things happened. Even Muslims would come to him for prayer. Because he could speak Arabic, he was able to communicate with Muslims in a way most Christians could not. So many people were now coming to Ibrahim that he realized God was calling him to do something with this gift of intercessory prayer.

And here's where the story gets interesting.

Ibrahim decided to go back to his home village and preach Jesus. He wasn't going to let little things like blindness and death sentences stop him. He paid a guy to put him on the back of the guy's motorbike and take him on the several-hour journey. When he got to the village, with only his clothes on his back, he wandered over to a shade tree, sat down, and started praying. Soon, as people saw this lonely-looking man sitting under a tree praying, they began approaching him and asking for prayers. Again healings and miracles began to happen. Within a year Ibrahim's family had become Christian. Shortly afterward the entire village was converted, and Ibrahim planted his first church. This blind, former Muslim sheik with a fatwa on his head planted a church in a Muslim village where his life had been threatened.

He smiled as he told me his story. My spine tingled.

Then he continued. Having converted his entire village to Jesus, Ibrahim decided that it was time for him to go plant another church. He paid another guy to take him on the back of a motorbike to another village, one Ibrahim had never visited. It too was 100 percent Muslim. Getting off the bike with nothing but the clothes on his back, Ibrahim again found a nearby shade tree, sat down, and began to pray. Within months the blind sheik had planted his second church.

When I met Ibrahim, he had done this six more times. The most recent church he planted was the result of hearing youths playing soccer. Wandering over to them, he asked if they were part of a league. They said no, and he offered to start a soccer league, which he did, in the process baptizing the entire soccer team and making contact with three more villages through their soccer teams—villages he will soon visit and also win to King Jesus.

When I sat with Ibrahim and heard his amazing story, tears welled up in my eyes. Here was this mystic—this saint—blind, happy, and in total and complete trust of Jesus Christ. He had given his life to Jesus, trusting him every single time he got on the back of a motorbike. He is the embodiment of an immersed life. He may be the most resolute, trusting human I've ever met. His final words as he told his story say it all: "I'm glad that I went blind, because if I hadn't gone blind, I would never have seen the light."

By drawing a line in the sand and standing up for King Jesus, this blind sheik is living a changed life. And he is changing the world. Forever.

MOSES' BASKET

Return with me to the story of Jenna and Dalton and their little girl. Their story has painful imagery, but Jenna and Dalton have opened their lives to the honor of King Jesus.

Evelynn was stillborn. Jenna and Dalton got to hold her, but only for a few minutes. Then staff members carried her little body off for a funeral. But all they had on hand to carry her away was a red bag. Jenna felt as though something was missing; it was her little girl, and all they could find for her was a bag.

So Jenna decided to use her pain to honor her king. There are thousands of stillborn babies every year. And so, there are thousands of parents who watch their little babies taken out of their birthing rooms forever. Shouldn't they have something special to carry such precious little babies in?

Jenna came up with an idea. Moses was rescued in a basket placed in the Nile. What if she began to provide baskets for stillborn babies? Baskets made with love and compassion. Baskets that communicate concern and empathy. Baskets that will handle such babies with the same kind of care baby Moses must have been given when placed in his basket.

So Jenna began a nonprofit ministry.[21] She provides beautiful baskets that honor babies. These are baskets that will allow parents an opportunity to see their beloved babies carried with love and grace. Jenna calls her ministry Evelynn's Baskets.

With every basket she gives, Jenna again demonstrates her faith in King Jesus. He will raise up every single person at the resurrection, including babies. Maybe I should say especially babies. And people who have followed King Jesus will be reunited with their families, including their babies, such as Evelynn.

When I first heard Jenna and Dalton's story, I knew I was hearing a story of profound faithfulness. And I knew that these are two people who trust in their king. I am so honored to know them that I can hardly describe it. And I want to be like they are. Faithful. Trusting. And immersed.

CHAPTER 7

OBEY THE TEACHINGS OF KING JESUS

"Teaching them to obey everything
I have commanded you."
—MATTHEW 28:20

Here's the thing about obedience: When we decide to obey King Jesus, we are not forced to serve using only our limited resources. He provides the opportunity and the power we need for obedience. He opens unexpected doors and provides the wind to sail through these doors.

Twenty-five years ago, I taught a two-week course in a Bible college in Seoul, Korea. I fell in love with the people of Korea, many of whom are orderly, respectful, and serious about learning from King Jesus. At the end of my two weeks there, I toured the city of Seoul and was taken to the Statue of Brothers.

The Statue of Brothers is a large monument that depicts two brothers on the battlefield, one from South Korea and the other from North Korea. They are standing in an emotional embrace on a dome that is cracked. It is a moving monument; the entire presentation is something of a prayer for the reunification of the country, which was divided, often along family lines, by a tragic war in the 1950s that few wanted.

I immediately thought of the millions of lost people who are basically imprisoned in North Korea. In the South, the kingdom of God is spreading, as there are hundreds of thousands of believers who are very serious about King Jesus. The largest church in the world is in Seoul. A few years ago, I had breakfast with its senior minister, Young Hoon Lee. He told me that once the dictatorial regime in the North falls, he has thousands of people ready to go into the North and witness to Jesus. But in the North, entire families are sentenced to labor camps merely for mentioning the name of Jesus. I have a hard time not wanting to go to North Korea and preach, regardless of the cost, though it is quite impossible to do so under the current regime.

When I was in Seoul, I worked with a minister whom I'll call Brother Jeong. He has the same passion for the North Koreans that I have. He has prayed for many years that God would open up a door for him to preach the good news in North Korea. He is willing to obey King Jesus and go there as soon as the door opens.

But just having the intention to obey has opened an odd and exciting door. Brother Jeong met a South Korean businessman who has family in North Korea that he hasn't seen in decades. This businessman too wanted to do something for the North Korean people. Working together, these two brothers came up with an idea. The businessman financed the printing of the gospel of Matthew on waterproof sheets of plastic, much like the plastic sheets used in small kitchen trash bags. Brother Jeong then attached the sheets of plastic to large helium balloons. He went up to the demilitarized zone in the late evening, and with the wind blowing northward, he released the balloons containing copies of the gospel into North Korea. Because the balloons have only enough helium to last an hour or so, thousands of copies of the gospel of Matthew have now been dropped all over North Korea.

The simple desire to obey King Jesus opened the door. And the last time I spoke with Brother Jeong, he asked my permission to download MPEGs of my sermons onto thumb drives and send them via helium balloons into North Korea. Imagine that: my sermons dropping all around the impoverished people of North Korea!

Because someone wanted to obey King Jesus. It's the power of obedience. Simply the intent to obey King Jesus will open unimaginable doors.

THE POWER OF OBEDIENCE

Jesus' final command in Matthew's gospel includes the instruction to teach people to obey everything Jesus has commanded the apostles.

In a democracy, we have become accustomed to designing our own laws. If we don't like the speed limit, we elect representatives who can change it. If we don't like the terms of a contract, we take the matter to court.

But in a kingdom, the king's word is the final authority for its subjects. A king doesn't put his decrees to a vote. If he is a good king, he considers what is true, what is good, and what is just, and then he issues his rulings on the basis of these. And he expects obedience.

This is of course the thesis of this book. We are called to respond to King Jesus with obedience-based discipleship.

Obedience has fallen on hard times in America. As one university student confessed to me, "I'm tired of other people telling me what to do." That sums it up for North Americans.

Some of us have downplayed obedience for theological reasons. We have wrongly confused obedience with works-righteousness or even legalism. Having been rightly taught that we are saved by faith alone, many of us have concluded that obedience can play no real part in salvation or even in following Jesus. Let me be clear here. We *are* saved by faith alone. We'll see in a moment that Jesus demands obedience. But we should never think that obedience is the means of salvation. It is not. Obedience is the sign that one has placed faith in Christ's rightness. It is the sign that we have truly repented and given up on our way and have instead embraced his way. Obedience is what faith looks like when it is faithful. Obedience is what faith looks like when it is, as Matthew Bates has convincingly argued, defined as allegiance to King Jesus.[22]

Imagine if your doctor told you that you have dangerously high blood pressure. She has monitored your health for years, and she knows you both as your doctor and as your friend. You have seen the readings. You know that you have a family history of heart disease. So she insists that you cut out salt and red meats, lose some weight, and begin taking blood pressure meds, for your own good.

What would faith look like in her office? Would you honestly be able to say that you have faith in her if you paid your bill and went back to your salty steaks?

Would you honestly be able to say you believe her if you didn't take your meds? Wouldn't you say that your faith was, in these scenarios, faithless?

King Jesus saves us through our faith in him alone. After all, what could we as broken humans possibly do to remove our own guilt? But the faith he expects is a faithful faith. It is a faith that is faithful enough to obey. As the brother of Jesus declares, any other faith is dead (James 2:17). He explains, "Someone will say, 'You have faith; I have deeds.' Show me your faith without deeds, and I will show you my faith by my deeds" (v. 18).

To argue, as Jesus does, that we should obey our king does not nullify the foundational principle of salvation by faith alone, for obedience is a demonstration of faith. The kind of faith Jesus seeks is faithful. It is obedient faith that King Jesus expects.

Hear King Jesus on the matter:

- "Anyone who loves me will obey my teaching. My Father will love them, and we will come to them and make our home with them" (John 14:23).
- "Very truly I tell you, whoever obeys my word will never see death" (John 8:51).
- "Everyone who hears these words of mine and puts them into practice is like a wise man who built his house on the rock. . . . But everyone who hears these words of mine and does not put them into practice is like a foolish man who built his house on sand" (Matt. 7:24, 26).

And there are more such Scriptures. Lots more.

So we must not misunderstand the biblical doctrine of salvation by faith alone in such a way as to suggest that obedience to our king is irrelevant. Nor should we confuse Jesus' call to obedience with legalism, the belief that one can earn heaven. Many of us require a theological adjustment in order to, as Hebrews says of King Jesus, learn obedience (Heb. 5:8).

But many more of us simply require the courage and commitment to stop rebelling against our king. That's because for many of us it is not a theological tenet that prevents us from prizing obedience. It is a rebellious spirit. In the garden of Eden, humanity fell on this very point. The evil one whispered in the ear of Eve, "Did God really say that?" And he has not stopped whispering it, even to this moment.

Let's say it clearly. When we embrace King Jesus and the kingdom of God, we must simultaneously embrace obedience-based discipleship. It is the imperative of the kingdom. And it is the only way to experience his life-giving blessings. We will find living, breathing proof in our own lives that the kingdom of God is real, powerful, beautiful, and here when we trust *and* obey King Jesus.

In a well-known thought experiment called the "Chinese room argument," offered to refute certain notions of artificial intelligence, philosopher John Searle posed an imaginary scenario. Allow me to adapt his experiment.

Imagine that a person is put into a blank room with a stack of cards that have certain markings on each. The person has no idea what the markings might mean (if anything). To him, they are just lines, dots, and serifs on a card. Now our man is given a set of instructions telling him to lay out the cards in a certain configuration, which he does.

Then a Chinese-speaking woman is brought into the room. Though the man had no idea of it, the markings on the cards are Chinese characters, and he has just arranged them—unbeknownst to him—in such a way as to create a beautiful poem in Chinese. The Chinese-speaking woman is moved. She weeps.

As with the man faced with cryptic symbols, some of the teaching of King Jesus can strike us with the uncertainty of foreign ideograms. Why would anyone want to turn the other cheek, refuse to store up treasures, or pray for their enemies? But here's the truth: King Jesus designed us, sustains us, and knows us intimately. He is like a father who knows his children far better than they know themselves. When we commit to obeying him, he creates a splendid poem of our lives, even if we don't at first understand it. This is the meaning of Paul's magnificent words in Ephesians 2:8–10, where he says that we are saved by grace to do good works: "We are God's handiwork"—the Greek word here is *poiēma*, related to our word *poem*—"created in Christ Jesus to do good works, which God prepared in advance for us to do" (v. 10). We obey the teachings of Jesus even when we don't fully understand them. And he creates a work of art in us because we did.

We should realize that the teachings of King Jesus cannot, in many cases, be understood apart from obedience.

Another philosophical illustration, this time borrowing from Frank Jackson. Imagine that a woman (Jackson calls her Mary) has lived her whole life in a white room in which every single object has been painted white, including herself. But Mary is a scientist, and her scientific specialty is color. Imagine that she knows everything there is to know about the color red. She knows how it affects the brain. She knows the exact measurements of its wavelengths. She knows how it is used in marketing, art, and social settings. There is nothing she doesn't know about the color red.

Except of course she really doesn't know red at all, for she has never experienced it. Who wouldn't say that any three-year-old who spies a red rose in the garden knows a thousand times more about the color red than Mary knows? It is often the experience of the thing that gives us our knowledge of it, not the study of it. We know things by experiencing them; in spiritual terms, we know things by doing them, not merely by reading about them. Obedience is the best teacher.

Like a color scientist in a monotone world, without obedience we might be able to know about praying for our enemies but still never really understand it. But when we pray for our enemies, we can experience the true joy that comes from handing burdens over to the Father in prayer. Through obedience—and only through obedience—we can have a deep and intimate knowledge of Jesus' teaching. Obeying a teaching is better than parsing it, in Greek, Hebrew, Latin, or any other language.

Here's another example. King Jesus teaches us that God joins one man and one woman in marriage and that we don't have the right to break this union. When we negotiate this teaching, try to discover ways out of it, or hire Greek professors to tell us it doesn't mean what it clearly says, we will never understand it. But when we are faithful to our spouses, work through our problems, and live up to our commitments, treating our spouses as God's provision for us, we can find the deep truth and beauty in what King Jesus teaches. We can discover the joy of being like Christ to our spouse, even when they may not deserve it.

King Jesus himself says that the best way to understand his teaching is through obedience: "Anyone who chooses to do the will of God will find out whether my teaching comes from God or whether I speak on my own" (John 7:17).

When I was a graduate student in religion, I studied under some of the world's best-educated Bible professors. One professor in my program was reportedly able to read as many as sixteen languages. He was a master at biblical studies and one of the most respected Bible scholars in the world. But he believed that much of the Bible was outdated, and he did not express much interest in obeying what the Bible teaches.

On the other hand, I have a contractor at my church who is earnest, hardworking, and devoted to King Jesus. I once preached a sermon based on Jesus' teaching about turning the other cheek, after which the contractor met me in the foyer and squared himself directly in front of me. At first I thought he was going to argue with me about the impossibility of obeying this text in his profession. He didn't. He said, "I want you to teach me how to obey this text. It sounds hard. But I want to do it."

The teaching is found in Matthew 5:39: "I tell you, do not resist an evil person. If anyone slaps you on the right cheek, turn to them the other cheek also." Question: who understands Matthew 5:39 better? The one who can read it in sixteen languages, teach the history of its interpretation, and describe the political, social, and psychological contexts of the text? Or the one who obeys it? My money is on the contractor, who through obedience will know a thousand times more about Matthew 5:39 than the scholar who has merely studied the verse.

THE ROLE OF THE APOSTLES' TEACHING

King Jesus' call for obedience is specific in Matthew 28:19–20. He doesn't simply say that we are to obey him. He says that we are to obey everything he has commanded the apostles: "teaching them to obey everything I have commanded you" (v. 20).

Jesus delegates authority to his apostles. He entrusts his truth to them as holy ambassadors. So when we read the writings of the apostles and their delegated prophets as contained in the Scriptures, we are hearing what Jesus commands. This makes the Bible the foundational document for obeying King Jesus.

Think about this a minute. Jesus never physically wrote a single book of the Bible (although he is the author behind each book). The only Christian witness we have of Jesus comes from those to whom he delegated the authority to compose the Bible. When Peter, Mark, Matthew, John, Jude, and Paul wrote Scripture, they were speaking with the authority of Jesus. This means that the only legitimate way to follow King Jesus is to follow what the Bible says. Without the Bible, you would know next to nothing about King Jesus. This is true for both Old and New Testaments, for Jesus accepted the authority of the Old Testament, and he explicitly commissioned the writing of the New. So we obey King Jesus when we obey the teachings of the sacred Scriptures.

It makes sense. Jesus himself was a man of the Bible, which contained only the Old Testament during his earthly ministry. Consider these examples of Jesus' acceptance of the Bible.

- Multiple times Jesus is presented as the embodiment of the Old Testament Scriptures (Matt. 1:1–17, 22–23; 2:5–6, 14–15, 17–18).
- Jesus himself declares that the Bible must be obeyed: "Do not think that I have come to abolish the Law or the Prophets; I have not come to abolish them but to fulfill them. For truly I tell you, until heaven and earth disappear, not the smallest letter, not the least stroke of a pen, will by any means disappear from the Law until everything is accomplished. Therefore anyone who sets aside one of the least of these commands and teaches others accordingly will be called least in the kingdom of heaven, but whoever practices and teaches these commands will be called great in the kingdom of heaven" (Matt. 5:17–19).
- Jesus teaches that Scripture cannot be broken (John 10:35).
- He calls the Scripture "the command of God" (Matt. 15:3).
- He refers to the written Bible as "the word of God" (Mark 7:13).

- He chastises the Sadducees for their partial disbelief of the Scriptures (Matt. 22:29–32).
- He answers the temptations of Satan by quoting the Bible (Matt. 4:1–11).
- He speaks about people and events of the written Scriptures as historic realities, such as Adam and Eve (Matt. 19:4), Cain and Abel (Luke 11:51), Noah (Luke 17:26), Jonah (Matt. 12:40), the creation account (Mark 10:6–9), and the reality of heaven and hell (Mark 9:45–48).

In each of these instances, Jesus shows us that the Scriptures of his day—the Old Testament Scriptures—constitute a sacred guide for disciples. After all, Jesus is none other than the God of the Old Testament. So King Jesus is the ultimate source of the Bible.

But Jesus goes farther. Jesus also ordains that his apostles continue writing the Bible, adding the New Testament to the Old. This means that the apostles and their delegates had the same kind of inspired authority as did the authors of the Old Testament. Speaking to the apostles, Jesus says, "When he, the Spirit of truth, comes, he will guide you into all the truth. He will not speak on his own; he will speak only what he hears, and he will tell you what is yet to come" (John 16:13). Jesus embraces the authority of the Old Testament. But he is also the authority behind the New Testament.

This explains why the writers of the New Testament thought they were writing Scripture. In Matthew 16:15–19, Jesus told the apostles that he would give them the keys of the kingdom: "Whatever you bind on earth will be bound in heaven, and whatever you loose on earth will be loosed in heaven" (v. 19). He called them to preach, to witness, and to lead the nations to obedience. For this reason, the apostles' names are inscribed on the foundations of the consummated kingdom (Rev. 21:14). The church is built on the foundation of the apostles and prophets (Eph. 2:19–21; the prophets are authorized delegates of the apostles). And the mysteries of Christ have been revealed today through the apostles and prophets (Eph. 3:4–5). Therefore Jesus explained that "if they obeyed my teaching, they will obey yours also" (John 15:20).

Peter calls the works of Paul Scriptures (2 Peter 3:15–16). Paul quotes from Luke and calls it Scripture (1 Tim. 5:18). Paul says that he got his message straight from God (2 Cor. 12:1–4; Gal. 1:11–12) and that God confirmed Paul's apostleship through signs, wonders, and powers (Rom. 15:18–19). He explains that the message he preached was not "a human word" but "the word of God, which is indeed at work in you who believe" (1 Thess. 2:13). And he states flatly that anyone who preaches any gospel different from the one he preached is damned by God (Gal. 1:8–9).

Peter describes how the Scriptures are inspired by the Spirit, since holy persons wrote as the Spirit carried them along (2 Peter 1:20–21). He reminds us that he did not invent what he wrote but was an eyewitness of the majesty of King Jesus (2 Peter 1:16). He explains that he is writing to stir up the minds of his readers: "I want you to recall the words spoken in the past by the holy prophets and the command given by our Lord and Savior through your apostles" (2 Peter 3:2). John goes so far as to threaten anyone who either adds to or takes away from the book he is writing, saying that adding to it will bring upon oneself the curses written in it, while taking away from it will cost you your life (Rev. 22:18–19).

Getting this right is life-giving. Getting it wrong, as the followers of every single fuzzy Jesus in chapter 3 do, robs us of the power King Jesus has to offer. Many of us have grown up in legalist environments where we fear that obedience to Scriptures will lead to legalism and judgmentalism. But legalism and judgmentalism are misreadings of Scripture. For the Scriptures are nothing less than a rich blessing. The Bible is, as the Psalms say, "a lamp for my feet, a light on my path" (Ps. 119:105). The Bible brings life. So obedience to the Scriptures is a beautiful and powerful thing.

Here's just one example.

Some time ago, I was counseling a woman who we'll call Sarah. One of her best friends—we'll call her Rita—had begun to put her down through things she said. Recently Rita said something particularly hurtful to Sarah. Sarah confessed to me that she had, in response, ceased all communications with Rita. Not being sure what had happened, Rita made repeated attempts to reach out to Sarah.

"I'm just so hurt by her I cannot talk to her," Sarah told me.

"What do the Scriptures teach you to do?" I asked.

"I know, I know," she responded. "But this is her fault. And it just hurts too much to think of speaking to her right now."

I advised her to pray about it and read what the Bible says about relationships. Some slights we forbear (Col. 1:13). Others call for forgiveness (Mark 11:25). And in some cases, we must work for reconciliation (James 5:19–20). "The teachings of Scripture are not a burden," I explained. "They are liberating. You know that you are the one in bondage here, don't you? And you don't have to be."

Eventually Sarah sat down with her friend. And to make a long story short, by talking lovingly and honestly with Rita, Sarah discovered that Rita had an entire world of hurt behind her that she had hidden for years. They opened up with each other. They cried together. They prayed together. And now their friendship is at a whole new level.

Free from bondage, Sarah got back in touch with me a couple weeks later. "You were right. Following the Scriptures set me free. But more than that. It is setting us both free."

THE TRUTH WILL SET YOU FREE

"I'm tired of people telling me what to do." That's the subtext of a million American lives. It sounds liberating, but it is really a form of bondage.

Years ago, North Americans worried that the dystopia George Orwell described in his novel *1984* would come true under some form of communist rule. If you haven't read *1984*, you've missed a classic. It gave us such terms as "thought crimes," "doublespeak," and "memory hole" as it wrestled with an imaginary world where everything a person does or thinks is monitored and controlled by big government.

Maybe government is too big or too controlling, but that's not the crisis that has overtaken most of us. Most of have succumbed not to Orwell's *1984* but to

Aldous Huxley's *Brave New World*. In Huxley's dystopian novel, people are not forcibly enslaved by a controlling government. Instead they voluntarily sell their freedom for a pleasure fix. In Huxley's world people are every bit as enslaved as in Orwell's world. But Huxley's slaves believe that unrestrained pleasure is true freedom. Nobody in Huxley's world ever excels, ever overcomes, or ever accomplishes anything. They are all shackled to their pleasures, like convicted prisoners.

Enslaved to doing it their way, nobody is truly free.

I can illustrate this by appealing to the football team of the University of Alabama (sorry, Auburn fans).

Apart from the astonishing and now-forgotten twenty-eight and twenty-seven national football championship titles held by Princeton and Yale, respectively (mostly from the 1800s), nobody can hold a candle to the Alabama Crimson Tide. They have seventeen national championships under their belts. Six of these were won under coach Nick Saban.

Now, I won't pretend to know everything there is to know about college football, but I know that Nick Saban runs a very tight ship. He hardly smiles. He is often angry with his players, snarling and scowling daily. He runs his team like a clock. When things don't go well, even if he is winning, he is not a happy man.

But people across the country line up to play for this five-foot-six giant of a man, because he *wins*. And he wins because he knows what he is doing and expects submission from his players. Saban doesn't invite his players to do their own thing. One hundred players on the field doing it their way wouldn't win a game, not even if they were competing against children. No, Saban has built a fantastic football program by expecting obedience. He disciplines his players to play the game well—to follow the rules, build strength and character, and adopt his incredible drive. Consequently, Saban wins, and he wins big.

The players for the Crimson Tide have not won championships by doing their own thing. It is by fully committing to the rules and the discipline of their leader that they have come to own the sport.

In the same way, obedience to King Jesus will give you the absolute best life you can have. He knows the game of life far better than you do. He can coach you from lostness to victory. He can bring out the best in you—in your emotions, your money, your body, your relationships, and your purpose. He is, after all, king of the universe. The precepts taught us by King Jesus are not oppressive, no more so than the disciplined football program brought to the Alabama players by Nick Saban is oppressive. The teachings of the Bible are structured, yes. But they are structured because they provide the very framework of a wonderful life. They are liberating. They are elevating. They make world-class humans of us. They set us free.

Allow me to give you a little coaching here about how to learn obedience to King Jesus.

John says that the commands of Jesus are not burdensome (1 John 5:3). That's true once we learn to love King Jesus. Is it burdensome to offer roses to a lover? Is it burdensome to take your child to Disney World? Is it burdensome to help a friend during a crisis? Not if you love them.

But love, like anything else, must sometimes be learned. It must be decided on, cultivated, honed, and built. Once we learn love, however, acting lovingly comes naturally.

So it is with obeying King Jesus. Start with discipline. Discipline is the art of requiring yourself to do something even when you don't feel like it. When you read a text of Scripture, discipline means that you will do it even if you don't feel like it. But here's the awesome thing about discipline: when it's exercised regularly, it leads to habit. Habits are what happen when your discipline begins to spin on its own, like a giant flywheel.

I started drinking coffee when I was in middle school, mostly to wake myself up in the mornings. I didn't like the flavor, but I did like the buzz. Soon, however, the regular discipline of drinking coffee led to a habit. A discipline requires tremendous effort, but a habit seems somewhat effortless. This is the case for any discipline—working out, reading, eating healthy, whatnot. After practicing a discipline long enough, we develop a habit. I am now a habitual coffee drinker.

And habits, when allowed to blossom, lead to character. When we speak of character, what we are describing is nothing other than one's habitual way of interacting with the world. You see, many of us think that we act according to our feelings. That's only half of the story. We also learn to feel according to our actions. If you run enough, you become a runner, and you feel the runner's high. If you love enough, you become a lover, and you feel the power of love. If you obey King Jesus enough, you become a Christ follower, and you feel his deep pleasure.

Character, when it fully blooms, leads to culture. Your culture is nothing other than your character played out over time. You will attract the future that your character reflects. We learned this at my church. When we made disciple making and church planting our main focus, we began to attract people who want to be disciple makers and church planters. We now have a culture of disciple making and church planting, and even if the top leadership were to leave, we would still do these things. It is now our culture, if not our destiny.

I started with the distasteful discipline of drinking coffee in the mornings just to wake up. But it led to a coffee habit. In forty years, I may have missed coffee only two or three days. Even when I fast, I generally allow myself a cup of coffee. And my habit has developed into something of a culture. For now, even though I have only one or two cups of coffee per day, it is among the most sublime things I do all day.

Obey King Jesus. Start with discipline. It will soon become habit. Then character. Then culture. Soon it will taste good. It will make sense. It will work. It will bring hope, peace, joy, and love. As King Jesus said, "Blessed . . . are those who hear the word of God and obey it" (Luke 11:28).

Every single fuzzy Jesus described in chapter 3 distorts obedience to King Jesus. Most of them consider obedience to be a burden, but to the contrary, it's liberating. What could give more freedom than living as you were designed to live?

In 2016, Armando Valladares was awarded the Canterbury Medal from the Beckett Fund for Religious Liberty. Valladares is a Christian who worked a desk in communist Cuba. When he was twenty-three years old, he was ordered to put a sign on his desk saying, "I am with Fidel"—a reference to the communist dictator of Cuba, Fidel Castro. Valladares had seen the murderous regime of Castro. As a Christian, Valladares refused to say he was with Fidel.

126

For this offense, Valladares was imprisoned for twenty-two years. "All of that time I endured hunger, systematic beatings, total darkness, filth, disease, sweltering heat, hard labor and solitary confinement. Eight thousand days of struggling to prove that I was a human being, eight thousand days of proving that my spirit could triumph over exhaustion and pain." His faith in Jesus, prayers, and memories of his church kept him alive, positive, and loving.[23]

To have succumbed to what he knew to be wrong would have constituted, he later said, spiritual suicide. To stand with Jesus was true freedom. "Even though my body was in prison and being tortured, my soul was free and it flourished. My jailers took everything away from me, but they could not take away my conscience or my faith."[24] That's what obedience to King Jesus does. It sets us free.

I once read a story about a guy who robbed a bank, stealing five thousand dollars. He was quickly apprehended, tried, and sent away to federal prison for years. Here's the crazy thing: though he didn't know it, the gun he used to rob the bank was a rare antique. If only he had sold the gun, he would have made twenty-five thousand dollars. And he could have freely spent the money on a thousand pleasures. Instead he threw away his life for five thousand dollars.

In your Bible, you have the sacred teachings of King Jesus, which are worth far more than anything else you might wish to follow. The teachings of Jesus are better than the mistruths of the world. Jesus' teachings will give you truth, freedom, and life. Don't just own them. Obey them.

CHAPTER 8

BEHOLD THE PRESENCE OF KING JESUS

"Surely I am with you always,
to the very end of the age."
—MATTHEW 28:20

Angels performing ballet. *Unbelievable,* I thought. *This can't be real.*

Here I was, lying on my side, wrapped around a tree like a koala bear, looking straight up into the eye of an EF4 tornado. And the debris at the top of the funnel looked just like angels gracefully performing ballet. During those few seconds in the eye of the tornado, I experienced the presence of King Jesus like never before or ever since. It felt transcendental and sweet.

Until the back wall of the tornado slammed against me, hurling two-by-fours, trees, and sheet metal at 180 miles per hour.

Here I was, caught completely exposed on a running trail in the middle of the most powerful tornado of 2009. It was Good Friday, and I was stressed out from preparing for a large Easter event on Sunday. We had spent weeks preparing for the day, and we were praying for two thousand people to attend, which would be a record for us.

What I needed, I concluded, was a good run. I have been a runner most of my life, and I typically use my running time for meditation, prayer, Scripture memorization, and stress relief. On this Friday, I decided to do a four-mile run on a greenway that runs along the Stones River in my hometown of Murfreesboro. It was about lunchtime, and I had decided to pray during the run that God would teach me to trust in him no matter what. As I ran, I was praying that God would let me behold that King Jesus is always with me.

So when it began to rain, I chuckled to myself and whispered a confident prayer to God: "No matter what storm comes, Lord, I know you are with me always." Soon the rain turned into hail. I kept running, surprised that the hail didn't hurt when it pelted me. Within a minute or two, however, lightning began to strike around me. Still a half mile from the car and out in the woods, I had no choice but to weather it out.

Every day for two months, I had been thinking about trusting King Jesus in extreme circumstances. *Here is my first test,* I thought. *Lightning may strike near me, but the Lord will provide.* "Okay, Lord," I prayed, "let's test my trust." I was pumped.

I left the trail and climbed down the bank to within a few feet of the river, crouching beneath some bushes and praying that the lightning wouldn't strike me. Suddenly, after four or five minutes, the rain and hail stopped. It was odd. The rain didn't slow down; it just stopped, all of a sudden. After ten minutes of lightning, rain, wind, and hail, the silence was disturbing. *But hey,* I thought, *at least the storm is over and I can continue running.* I stood up to climb back onto the trail.

When I stood up, however, something didn't seem right. To this moment, I cannot say what I felt, but I knew in my gut that something was wrong. I couldn't see much of the sky. I could see the trail, which was about eye level, and I could see the wooded slope leading up to the parking lots, but I couldn't see the horizon beyond that. In the distance I heard a low rumble, which was getting louder.

At this point, you might expect me to say that I was terrified, but I wasn't really scared. Events were unfolding too quickly for me to feel much fear. Besides, I had been talking to God for forty minutes about trusting that he is always with me. So rather than fear, I felt this intense sense of challenge; I told myself that whatever was coming my way would strengthen my faith. I felt a bizarre sense of appreciation to God.

The rumble was very loud by now, and I heard cars honking, metal screeching, and transformers exploding. "Dude," I said jokingly to myself, still not sure what was going on, "you're in a tornado. God is going to give you the ultimate test. You're going to learn trust, in a crazy, crazy way."

I had five seconds to decide what to do.

I quickly looked around at the options: bunches of trees, the river, a small dock in the water. Nothing else. The nearest tree of noteworthy size was a few feet away. I quickly wrapped my arms around it, laid on the ground, curled my body around the trunk, and looked up to monitor the situation. I asked God to forgive me of my sins, then mumbled something like, "Let's get going!"

Within two seconds I saw the first pieces of debris flying over me. They were topping the trees above the trail, coming from the direction of the parking lots as though shot from a cannon. Then I heard the cracking of wood, not a little bit but the sound of an entire forest being split at once. It is not a sound that you can ever forget—wood from a whole forest violently exploding. If you can imagine ten thousand baseball bats being broken at the same time, you will know what I heard. I checked my grip on the tree and thought, *Here it is!*

Immediately afterward, I saw the wall of the tornado top the crest of the slope and slam into me. The sound was amazing, and the power incredible. Everything around me, including the ground, was shaking. I could feel my tree groaning as it was trying to leave the ground. The whole forest heaved. Debris was crashing all around me. Static electricity made my hair stand on end. I saw what appeared to be a house fly right over my head, past the river, and off into the wild. I was in the strongest tornado to touch down anywhere in the U.S. that year; it cut a path twenty-three miles long. And at this moment the tornado was at its very worst. According to witnesses interviewed later, the tornado paused right on top of me, grinding its fury into the forest, the river, and my fully exposed body.

Though I had curled myself around the tree, the tornado picked up my legs and extended my body into the wind. I suppose my adrenaline was working properly, because I never lost grip of the tree, even though my body was now off the ground, flapping in the wind like a flag. I never thought I'd lose my grip; I was determined that I would not fail this test. I wanted to make God proud of me. I kept thinking that I needed to document the experience in my mind so I could help others. I never closed my eyes.

The front wall of the tornado pulverized the forest around me, but when it passed, I found myself in the strangest world I've ever seen. I was in the eye of the tornado, and I knew it. I dropped back to the ground and instinctively curled around the tree again. A lot of debris was still shooting across the river, firing across my line of sight like meteors. But now I also saw debris spiraling inside the vortex of the tornado. Close to me, it was traveling at lightning speed, racing around and around just like you'd expect.

But farther up, along the inside of the funnel, the debris was moving slowly, gracefully, almost playfully at the top. It wasn't circling; it was dancing, up and down more than side to side, like angels dancing in ballet. A strange light illuminated the inside of the tornado. It was surreal. It was peaceful, calm, and full of the presence of Jesus.

It is impossible to describe the feelings you get in the eye of a tornado. There is such a mixture of primal feelings—blood pulsing, mouth drying, eyes focused, heart racing, muscles taut. Everything that has been you, in my case for forty-eight years, comes down to one timeless point and freezes; your breathing calms, and your mind seems to step out of your body and look around in amazement. You notice the smallest details: a leaf blowing past, a small sound, the strange illumination inside the vortex. You watch the inside of the funnel as though you were watching a movie. There's a strange sense of detachment.

And I felt, at the same time, both all alone and immersed in the love of God. In the eye of the storm there is no one else, and as far as I could tell, the entire world was now gone. Nothing looked familiar, and I had the sense that I had already died and gone to heaven. I felt loved in the eye of that tornado, and even now the recollection of that feeling moves me to tears.

Eventually, however, the back wall of the tornado struck, and it was even more violent than the front. It uprooted hundreds of trees around me. They launched straight up from the ground like missiles, then fell back down all around me. Two trees landed on top of me; I saw them crash into me, but oddly, I didn't feel them. The grinder then moved on.

As soon as the tornado passed, I managed to crawl out of the devastation with a broken leg and a deep gash on my head, covered with blood and mud. But I was alive. And I was excited. I had asked God to give me the kind of trust that would forever banish fear. King Jesus had promised always to be with me; I wanted to trust in that truth. And in the Good Friday tornado of 2009, I learned how.

When Easter rolled around that Sunday, I was able to stand among the lilies arranged across the stage and proclaim to my congregation that King Jesus is truly with us. *Always*. And 2,307 people were there to hear the message.

So when I say that Jesus is present with us always, you can be sure that I have experienced it in my own life. He is always with us.

FOUR MIRACLES BEFORE BREAKFAST

The final words of King Jesus in Matthew's gospel offer us the hope, reassurance, and power of the constant and unending presence of King Jesus: "Surely I am with you always, to the very end of the age" (Matt. 28:20). The Greek term translated in the NIV as "surely" literally means "look" or "behold!" This final chapter of the book will explore the beauty of seeing King Jesus in our lives. In the Good Friday tornado of 2009, I beheld Jesus' constant presence. But you can behold it every single day, in a million different ways.

It is this abiding presence of King Jesus that makes every other mandate of Matthew 28:18–20 work. Who are we to make disciples of all nations? Who are we to immerse people in a relationship with the king? Who are we to muster the power of obedience? Without the power and presence of King Jesus, we could do none of these things. And if we try to do them without his power and presence, we will find ourselves frustrated, exhausted, and gloomy. The abiding presence of King Jesus is the source of strength that makes everything else in his final command possible.

To explore how we are to behold the presence of King Jesus, let's talk a little about miracles.

In 1776, the enormously influential Scottish philosopher David Hume died. Hume is important because, among other things, he dealt with questions of nature, skepticism, and epistemology—how we come to know things.

Hume was something of an atheist, and in his efforts to undermine Christian claims of miracles, he developed a definition of miracles that is wrong but which stuck with Westerners. Even Christians adopted Hume's definition of miracles. Hume argued that a miracle occurs whenever God works contrary to the laws of nature. Using complex arguments, Hume insisted that we can prove no instance of any god working contrary to the laws of nature. So he concluded that there are no miracles—or at least we can no longer speak about miracles.

Whenever you let an unbeliever define your terms, you are going to have problems. Ever since Hume, Western Christians have accepted a definition of miracles that limits them to things contrary to the laws of nature. We then wrongly suggest that most of what God does today is mere providence, by which we mean "things according to nature." Such a distinction, however, is unbiblical, for the authors of the Bible did not distinguish between things contrary to nature and things through nature, and such a bifurcated view of the work of God frequently devolves into a belief that God rarely does anything at all in our world. As a consequence, many Christians have lived unable to see King Jesus' powerful presence, which is at work everywhere and all of the time. And this inability to behold Jesus leaves us alone, empty, and powerless.

Without a robust view of the work of God that permeates all of life, we will miss the beautiful and powerful things King Jesus is doing right here and right now. A stunted view of the ongoing work of God has left millions of disciples with a form of faith but without its power (2 Tim. 3:5). We are like spiritual automobiles that have no engines. It's sad, lonely, and frustrating to try to follow King Jesus without depending on his power.

What would happen if we returned to the biblical definition of miracles? In the Bible, we don't read of things contrary to nature versus things through nature. We would read the biblical terms of "signs, wonders, and powers" (Heb. 2:4, my translation) and discover that King Jesus has never stopped doing these things. He still does "signs," things that point to other things (such as himself!). He still does "wonders," things that make your jaw drop (like living through an EF4 tornado). And he still does "powers," commanding situations with extraordinary might.

If he didn't still do these things, we would be all on our own in following him. And he wouldn't be much of a king.

We should be experiencing the work of God every day of our lives. Whether or not we acknowledge it, we are already experiencing signs, wonders, and powers. But our theology may be preventing us from recognizing them. Every good gift comes down from the Father (James 1:17). When grass grows, it is a work of God (Ps. 104:14). When we eat our bread and drink our wine, these are given us by the power of God (Ps. 104:14–15). When nations rise and fall, this is the work of God (Acts 17:26). And he still offers us healing and well-being (Mal. 4:2).

The book of Revelation confirms that King Jesus is still doing signs, wonders, and powers among us. In Revelation, there are three cycles of sevens: a cycle of Jesus opening the seven seals of a scroll, a cycle of seven trumpets being blown by angels, and a cycle of seven bowls of wrath being poured out. The important thing to note in these cycles is how each releases an event on earth under the control of heaven. Every time Jesus breaks a seal in heaven, the earth responds. Every time a trumpet sounds around the throne of God, a disaster occurs on earth. And every time a bowl is poured out from heaven, the earth shakes. The message is clear. Heaven's kingdom is now controlling earth's destiny. And Jesus is there, directing it alongside the Father.

The problem for most of us occurs when we come to believe that it's a miracle only if two plus three equals six. And of course that would be a miracle. But there is a much more common miracle available to us. It occurs when two plus three equals five, but we had neither the two nor the three necessary to get five. A miracle occurs when we have nothing and King Jesus gives us the two and three we need to get our five.

And that leads me to Adam.

God could create fifty thousand dollars from thin air and drop it into your lap. But he seems to prefer that we participate in the miracle, so he often supplies us with the fifty thousand dollars we need by leading others to join the miracle by way of their generosity. This is true even if you are a teenager like Adam.

Adam is a member of my church. He had heard about an important ministry to children in a midsize city in Tanzania. It's a children's home that cares for orphans, children in deep poverty, and albinos, who in this culture are sometimes killed because of superstition. The children's home was started by some friends of mine who could no longer watch children die in the poverty-stricken northern part of Tanzania. They care for the world's poorest in the name of King Jesus.

My wife, Julie, is on the board of the children's home. Only a few months ago, the board recognized the need to expand the children's home because there are so many children among the people in need. But they had no money. Julie called together ten friends and asked them to fast and pray for a week that God would supply them with the sixty thousand dollars they needed to build an additional home for children who age out of the program but have no place to go. Within a week, even though not a single person was asked for money, sixty thousand dollars was given to them. God did not create it out of thin air. He did better. He created it out of the hands and hearts of his people.

But that's not all. The children's home also provides formula for newborn babies whose mothers are too malnourished to supply milk. There are many such mothers. The formula can cost as much as three days' wages, which is not an option for hundreds of mothers who live in extreme poverty. When the children's home ran out of money for more formula, Julie again decided to pray. But this time she asked Adam to join her in fasting and prayer. Adam is part of a homeschooling family of disciples, and Julie has been teaching him a few hours per week for several years. Adam is a kindhearted young man. When he heard about the need to care for these babies, he wanted to help. But the children's home needed fifty thousand dollars to buy enough formula for the next year and a half, in addition to the sixty thousand dollars they already had raised.

Adam approached our youth minister to ask if he could make an announcement to the other teens about the campaign to raise support for the formula, and take up a collection for it. The youth minister gladly agreed and even said he would match whatever was given, up to five hundred dollars. They expected a couple hundred dollars; these were teens, after all.

Adam didn't have a job; he was only sixteen. But he decided to give twenty dollars himself. And then he prayed.

On the night of the collection, the youth group gave sixteen hundred dollars. The youth minister added his five hundred dollars. Just before the offering, totally separate from each other, two sets of parents also offered to give five hundred dollars each. Then another parent promised to match whatever the youth gave. Now Adam's small collection had gone from several hundred dollars to forty-seven hundred dollars. Then a local company heard about the initiative and offered to match the total offering. Forty-seven hundred dollars became ninety-four hundred dollars. Another teenager went to her school and decided to raise more funds, getting the whole school in on the act. And as if this weren't enough of a miracle, someone contacted Adam and Julie after it was all over and whispered that he was selling some property and would, in his words, "make sure they got the whole fifty thousand dollars."

This is a miracle, but it is a miracle in which hundreds of people got to join in and become part of the awesome thing our king is doing. Maybe dropping fifty thousand dollars into Adam's lap would have been more showy, but offering three hundred people the chance to save a life in the name of King Jesus is obviously closer to the heart of God.

And this miracle isn't one of only a few miracles that you might read about in some dusty history book. This happened only a few weeks before I wrote this paragraph. Somewhere in an impoverished city in Tanzania, a desperate woman who could make no milk prayed this prayer: "Lord, please save my child!" And somewhere else, eight thousand miles away, God gave a couple of disciples $110,000 through nothing but prayer, fasting, and the hands of people willing to become part of a miracle. Maybe two plus three didn't equal six. But if you were the mother in Tanzania who had neither a two nor a three, $50,000 worth of formula is a pretty good miracle.

I see such miracles all the time, because I know lots of people who are committed to obedience to King Jesus and to beholding his presence, as the final sentence of Matthew's gospel teaches us to do. "Behold, I am with you always" (28:20, my translation).

Only a week before writing this chapter, I was talking to one of our deacons.

He is a part-time staff member who guarantees that at our church if you need a pastoral visit, you'll get one quickly and lovingly. I recently had surgery done on my knee. Sitting in the waiting room with him early the morning of my surgery, I asked him how it was going.

He told me about four powerful and loving acts of King Jesus that he had witnessed among the members of our church over the last couple of months. A newborn was taken off life support, which had been necessitated by meningitis, after prayers of healing and anointing with oil (an intensified form of prayer, according to James 5:14). A woman with a hemorrhage (specifically, a deadly case of hematoma) recovered after some of our members laid hands on her (as Jesus did in Mark 10:13, 16) and prayed. A dying member of my church was taken off hospice care after a group went and laid hands on him. And a man with cancer was declared cancer free after six months of treatment and intense prayers by the church.

Four miracles before breakfast. Not bad.

What if you lived every day fully expecting the work of God? What would change in your life if you learned that every good thing that happened is from God and if you learned to seek the work of God in every place in your life? What would it look like if you beheld the presence of King Jesus in obedience-based discipleship?

I'm not arguing that you should be able to walk on water (though if God allows it, I'm for it). Nor am I arguing that God physically heals everyone who prays; I have personally prayed, fasted, and wept over numerous sick people who were not healed, at least not physically. And I'm certainly not arguing that we should believe every person who claims to perform miracles. There have been plenty of frauds out there, and we must practice discernment. Even the devil masquerades as an angel of light (2 Cor. 11:14).

What I am arguing is that every good gift you experience, whether it comes through the hands of a doctor, a sturdy storm shelter, or a generous friend, ultimately comes from King Jesus. Go back to Matthew 28:20. King Jesus doesn't just say, "I am with you always." He says, "Behold, I am with you always." I am arguing that you should look for and behold the presence of King Jesus. If you behold it, you will find it. Everywhere. And when you do, everything else in the final words of Matthew's gospel will spring to life. You'll have love. You'll have purpose. You'll have joy. You'll make disciples. You will not be left on your own to do the impossible.

Behold the everywhere presence of King Jesus, and you'll have life.

JESUS IS A FAITHFUL KING

The apostle Paul regularly uses the term "in Christ." It is among his favorite ways of speaking about discipleship. Here's just one instance: "Now it is God who makes both us and you stand firm in Christ. He anointed us, set his seal of ownership on us, and put his Spirit in our hearts as a deposit, guaranteeing what is to come" (2 Cor. 1:21–22). This is Paul's way of reassuring us that we have not been left alone on our road of discipleship. We get to live in Jesus, under his anointing, and sealed with his Spirit.

So we live our entire lives in Christ. When Jesus calls us to live as disciples, he also equips us to do the work of discipleship. King Jesus doesn't just ask *us* for faith. He proves, over and over again, that he is also faithful to us. "God is faithful, who has called you into fellowship with his Son, Jesus Christ our Lord" (1 Cor. 1:9).

Steve Patterson is a high school basketball coach who is deeply committed to King Jesus. He has been discipling high school and university students for years. He gathers them together, sometimes fifteen, twenty, or thirty at a time, and leads them to make radical decisions for Jesus. I've met some of his disciples. They also are deeply committed to King Jesus. It makes my heart sing to see what they're doing.

I had coffee with Steve and four of his disciples last summer and listened to how they are changing their schools for King Jesus. Then they mentioned to me that they were also sponsoring a disciple-making house in Nepal (of all places!).

They had found out about Nepal through some travels that Steve does in making disciples internationally. These sixteen-, eighteen-, and twenty-year-olds wanted to build a house in Nepal that could be used as a launching pad for bringing many others to King Jesus. There were only two problems. First, they knew that the Christian faith is often unwelcome in this "roof of the world" nation. Second, they needed eighteen thousand dollars to build the house.

As I listened to the teenagers speak, I asked them if they believe in miracles. Several said yes and that they had been praying for a miracle for Nepal. I told them that my congregation also believes that when we obey King Jesus, he miraculously supplies our needs.

"Come to my church this Sunday," I said. "Let's see if God gives us a miracle."

The following Sunday, Steve and several students came to one of our services. Coincidentally, it was a Back-to-School Sunday at our church, so we were planning to host a lunch for all the returning students from our local university, MTSU.

I don't remember what I preached that Sunday, but somewhere in the middle of the sermon, I had Steve and his students stand up. I told my congregation who they were and what they were doing locally. I told my church that they were building a house in Nepal for discipleship and prayer. I didn't ask for a penny. Then I just mentioned to my church that Steve and his crew were looking for a miracle.

Within thirty minutes I had eight thousand dollars. By Tuesday of that week, I had eighteen thousand dollars—everything they needed to build the house. They had their miracle, and I never once asked for a penny.

But King Jesus also does add touches of grace, just to make the wonder more wonder-full.

Right after the Sunday services, my church had its lunch for university students. I invited Steve and his students to come to lunch with me. Steve was holding thousands of dollars that had just been handed them. We wandered back into the fellowship hall, now filled with two hundred people. We sat down with three who we assumed were university students. I introduced myself to them.

Then they introduced themselves. Two were medical doctors, and another was a PhD. Then, to my utter amazement, they told us that all three were visiting that day from—get this—*Nepal*, and they were attending North Boulevard for the very first time. You can't make this stuff up.

You may think that this is a chapter on miracles, but it is not. Not really. It is instead a chapter on the ongoing presence of King Jesus and the beauty of beholding that presence. We do it through prayer. We do it through Bible study. We do it through having the eyes of our hearts opened by him. He has made an enormous promise: "Behold, I am with you always, to the very end of the age." This is a chapter on beholding.

When King Jesus, wearing a crown of thorns and a purple robe, was presented by Pilate to the angry mob, Pilate said, "Behold the man!" (John 19:5, my translation). Before Jesus ascended to the right hand of the throne of God, he said, "Behold, I am with you always." I encourage you to open your eyes and see the king who is here. For when we offer our full allegiance to him, when we crown him king of our lives, and when we commit to obedience-based discipleship, he does amazing things.

Before I end this book, allow me to tell one more story about my son.

Jonathan was born with a condition called metopic craniosynostosis. The bones in his skull were fused together, leaving no room for his brain to develop. Fifty years ago, it would have killed him. But thanks to amazing advances in medicine, today there is a surgery to fix the condition. Jonathan was scheduled to have the surgery at six months of age. It requires two surgeons. They cut the skull into pieces, screw them together with appropriate gaps, and then stitch it all back together again. It is a form of brain surgery. And just as the condition is life-threatening, so is the surgery.

The night before the surgery, every one of my elders showed up at our house to pray for my son and anoint him with oil (as James 5:14 teaches). I'll never forget the feeling I had when one of the most godlike men I've ever known lathered up his hands with olive oil, slathered it all over my son's head, and begged God to heal him. All twelve elders laid their hands on him, knelt on the floor, and prayed.

The next day, Jonathan was in a six-hour surgery. Julie and I waited and prayed. We had been warned that after the surgery Jonathan's head would swell beyond the point of recognition. His eyes would swell shut. And it would be some time before we would know if the surgery had helped. "If, after the swelling goes down, he reaches for a Cheerio," the neurosurgeon said, "that will suggest that he still has healthy brain function."

My wife, who has been quite a prayer warrior through the years, prayed a simple prayer. "Lord, please heal our son so completely that one day he leads prayer at church." She must have prayed this prayer a thousand times.

He came out of the surgery looking horrible. It's too emotional for me to describe, but we weren't sure he would ever speak again. Or even live.

But after a week, the swelling went down. He started to rouse. I vividly remember his first smile; with his eyes still swollen shut, he responded to my voice.

Soon after coming home, I began putting Cheerios in front of him, waiting to see if he would reach for one. For several days he just stared at them. And then, a couple days after the swelling subsided, my son reached out and picked up a Cheerio. I shouted for joy. He smiled before eating the entire pile.

The years went by, and we forgot the specific prayer that Julie and I had prayed, though we've never forgotten the deep pain of Jonathan's condition. Life moved on. We moved to Kansas City and began working for a church there.

Then, in the spring of 2005, Jonathan asked me to baptize him. It was one of the happiest days of my life. Two weeks later I was scheduled to give a keynote address at the Pepperdine University Bible Lectures. It was spring break, so I took Jonathan with me.

Just before I got up to speak, the director of the lectures asked me to appoint someone to say a prayer after my speech. I hadn't been aware that this was part of my responsibility as the speaker, and I hardly knew anyone there. So I mentioned to the director that my son had just been baptized. "Let Jonathan say the prayer," I said without much thought.

I don't know exactly how many people were in the assembly that day, perhaps around five thousand. My lesson was ho-hum. It was the first time I had ever been on jumbo screens, and to be honest, I was distracted by them.

I sat down. Jonathan went up on the stage. Then King Jesus showed me one of the most glorious evidences of his presence I've ever witnessed.

When I looked up in the venue at Pepperdine that day, I remembered the prayer that Julie and I had prayed to God about our son during his surgery: "Lord, please heal our son so completely that one day he says a prayer in church." I beheld my son on the jumbo screens. He opened his mouth in the very first prayer he had ever said in church.

And there, before five thousand people, King Jesus proved his faithfulness to me. My son, the one who should have died from his condition, said his first prayer not just in church. He said his prayer in front of the whole wide world.

That's faithfulness.

That's something to behold.

That's King Jesus!

NOTES

1. Wright has published numerous works on Jesus as king and on the kingdom of God, but the most accessible is *How God Became King: The Forgotten Story of the Gospels* (San Francisco: HarperOne, 2012). Scot McKnight's most accessible book is *The King Jesus Gospel: The Original Good News Revisited*, rev. ed. (Grand Rapids: Zondervan, 2016).
2. J. C. Wallace, "Hymn for Young Children," in *A Collection of Hymns for Public and Private Worship*, ed. John R. Beard (London: John Green, 1838), 301.
3. For other Scriptures that in some way or another affirm the deity of King Jesus, see Isaiah 9:6–7; Daniel 7:13–14; John 8:58; 10:32–33; 20:27–28; Acts 20:28; Romans 9:5; Titus 2:11–14; Hebrews 1:8; 2 Peter 1:1; 1 John 5:20.
4. John Baxter, *Missing: Believed Killed* (Aurum Press, 2010).
5. Ron Sider, *The Scandal of the Evangelical Conscience* (Grand Rapids: Baker, 2005), 12.
6. Tertullian, *Apologeticus*, chapter 50.
7. To borrow from the title of Tullian Tchividjian's work *Jesus + Nothing = Everything*, 2nd ed. (Wheaton: Crossway, 2011).
8. For extensive evidence of this, see my book *A Grand Illusion* (Nashville: Renew, 2019).
9. Chris Higgins, "Sixty-Four People and Their Famous Last Words," MentalFloss.com, *http://mentalfloss.com/article/58534/64-people-and-their-famous-last-words* (accessed February 27, 2019).
10. Jesus Diaz, "Woman Drives for 900 Miles Instead of Ninety Thanks to GPS," Gizmodo.com, *https://gizmodo.com/woman-drives-for-900-miles-instead-of-90-thanks-to-gps-5975787* (accessed March 25, 2019).

11. Sean McDowell, "What If Everyone Lived the Sexual Ethic of Jesus?" SeanMcDowell .com, *https://seanmcdowell.org/blog/what-if-everyone-lived-the-sexual-ethic-of-jesus* (accessed March 30, 2019).

12. Ibid.

13. See Jim Putman, *Church Is a Team Sport: A Championship Strategy for Doing Ministry Together* (Grand Rapids: Baker, 2009).

14. *Christian Heroes and Martyrs* (Philadelphia: Charles Foster), 41.

15. Bobby Harrington, *Trust and Follow Jesus: Conversations to Fuel Discipleship* (Nashville: Renew, 2019).

16. FinalCommand.com, *www.finalcommand.com* (accessed April 6, 2019).

17. For another excellent resource for a discipleship group, see Bobby Harrington, *Trust and Follow Jesus: Conversations to Fuel Discipleship* (Renew.org, 2019).

18. Maritza and Juan Carillo, "A Group of People in Houston Form a Human Chain to Rescue a Man Trapped in an SUV Submerging in Water," CNN.com, *www.cnn.com /videos/weather/2017/08/30/human-chain-harvey-rescue-ath.cnn* (accessed April 5, 2019).

19. Tony Twist, Bobby Harrington, and David Young, *Baptism: What the Bible Teaches* (Nashville: Renew, 2018).

20. Jim Putman and Bobby Harrington, *Discipleshift: Five Steps That Will Help Your Church Make Disciples Who Make Disciples* (Grand Rapids: Zondervan, 2013), 20.

21. I urge you to visit Jenna's website at *evelynnsbasket.com*.

22. See Matthew Bates, *Salvation by Allegiance Alone: Rethinking Faith, Works, and the Gospel of Jesus the King* (Grand Rapids: Baker Academic, 2017).

23. Angelo Stagnaro, "Armando Valladares, Imprisoned and Tortured by Castro, Awarded Canterbury Medal," NationalCatholicRegister.com, *www.ncregister.com/blog/astagnaro /armando-valladares-honored-for-refusing-a-pinch-of-incense-to-castro* (accessed April 4, 2019).

24. Ryan Colby, "Armando Valladares Speech Transcript: Armando Valladares Receives the 2016 Canterbury Medal," BecketLaw.org, *www.becketlaw.org/media/armando -valladares-speech-transcript/* (accessed April 4, 2019).

David Young completed an MA at Harding School of Theology and an MA and PhD in New Testament at Vanderbilt University. He has worked for churches in Missouri, Kansas, and Tennessee, taught at several universities, and spoken around the world. He is the host of the *New Day* television program and author of several books, including *The Rhetoric of Jesus in the Gospel of Mark* (Fortress, 2017), coauthored with Michael Strickland, and *A Grand Illusion* (Renew, 2019). David is a cofounder of Renew, a movement that renews the teachings of Jesus to fuel disciple making. He currently serves as the senior minister for the North Boulevard Church in Murfreesboro, Tennessee. David and his wife, Julie, have two children, each married to great spouses.